FAMILY AND CONSUMER SCIENCE LIFEPAC

WHAT'S COOKIN'?

CONTENTS

Author:	**Marcia Parker, M.Ed.**
Editor:	Alan Christopherson, M.S.
Illustrations:	Alpha Omega Graphics

Alpha Omega Publications®

804 N. 2nd Ave. E., Rock Rapids, IA 51246-1759

WHAT'S COOKIN'?

The kitchen is one of the most important rooms in the home. More time is spent in your kitchen than any other room. It is important to make sure that your kitchen is set up for efficient, fun, and safe use. This LIFEPAC® will introduce you to the most popular and effective kitchen layouts, large and small equipment used for ease of food preparation and storage, and names and uses of kitchen utensils. Since safety in the kitchen is extremely important, this LIFEPAC will also address this topic as well.

When cooking, the first step is to have the right amounts of the right ingredients. Learning what to look for in a recipe and how to read a recipe is very important. The second section of LIFEPAC 2 will teach you how to read and use recipes more proficiently.

Before you start to cook, there are some important things you should consider. You need to think about your food budget and where to shop for the best bargains. You should learn how to read labels so that you purchase wisely, economically, and nutritionally. When purchasing food, storage must be considered also. These aspects of cooking are designated as meal management. Once you gain an understanding of each of these areas, you will be ready to proceed to meal planning and food preparation.

OBJECTIVES

Read these objectives. The objectives tell you what you will be able to do when you have successfully completed this LIFEPAC.

When you have completed this LIFEPAC, you should be able to:

1. Identify and describe the most popular and effective kitchen layouts.
2. Identify the names and uses for equipment and utensils found in the kitchen.
3. Gain an understanding for safety in the kitchen.
4. Identify what to look for in a good recipe and how to read a recipe.
5. Identify cooking terms, equivalents, abbreviations, and measurements found in recipes.
6. Identify the different aspects of meal management.
7. Demonstrate skill in maintaining a food budget through careful buying strategies.
8. Compare and contrast different types of food stores.
9. Demonstrate supermarket etiquette.
10. Identify nutritional and economic values from reading good labels.
11. Gain an understanding of various methods of proper food storage.
12. Explain the importance of proper food storage.

Note: All vocabulary words in this LIFEPAC appear in **boldface** print the first time they are used. If you are unsure of the meaning when you are reading, study the definitions given.

I. GETTING ACQUAINTED WITH THE KITCHEN

Whether warm and cozy or sleek and sculptured, your kitchen is the most important room in your house. It is also probably the most expensive to equip. More elements—appliances, fixtures, plumbing, wiring, and furniture—fit into a given space in the kitchen than anywhere else in your home. More time is spent in the kitchen than anywhere else in the home as well. It is important that you are familiar with the variety in layouts, the necessary equipment used and the safety involved in your kitchen. This section will introduce these aspects of getting acquainted with your kitchen.

SECTION OBJECTIVES

Review these objectives. When you have completed this section, you should be able to:

1. Identify and describe the most popular and effective kitchen layouts.
2. Identify the names and uses for equipment and utensils found in the kitchen.
3. Gain an understanding of safety in the kitchen.

TYPES OF UNIT KITCHENS

The three major kitchen elements (sink, stove, and refrigerator) form what kitchen designers call a work triangle. The shape is defined by drawing a line between these elements. Here are the recommended dimensions, according to the National Kitchen and Bath Association:

- Each side of the work triangle should be four to seven feet long.

- There should be two feet of workspace on either side of the sink.

- The dishwasher should be near the sink—next to it, preferably.

- There should be at least 18 inches of food preparation space near the refrigerator and at least 18 inches space on both sides of the stove.

More trips are made around this triangle than to any other area of the kitchen so it is important that the distance between them lends itself to efficiency. The ideal arrangement is to place the sink between the range and the refrigerator with a work surface on either side.

The most common kitchen layouts are similar to the basic ones shown in the illustrations below.

SAMPLE LAYOUTS AND WORK TRIANGLES

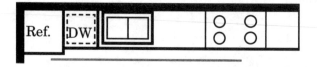

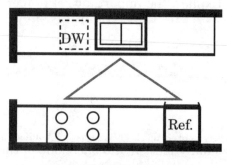

ONE COUNTER   CORRIDOR

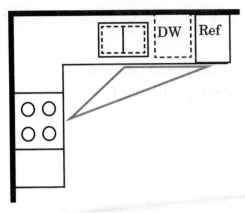

L-SHAPED

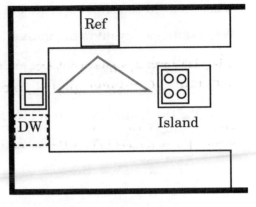

U-SHAPED WITH ISLAND

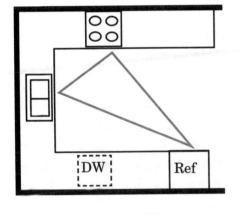

U-SHAPED

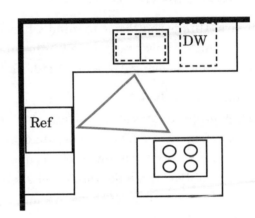

L-SHAPED WITH ISLAND

The U-shaped layout is generally the most efficient because the equipment and cabinets are grouped on three sides of the kitchen with the sink in the center of the U. This obviously has the best work triangle space. The L-shaped layout ranks second in efficiency. The equipment and cabinets are placed on two adjacent sides. When possible, the sink and the range are placed at right angles to one another. This layout saves steps and, consequently, time, and energy. The corridor or two-wall kitchen requires more steps and has space limitations. The equipment and cabinets are on two parallel walls in this layout. The one-counter or one-wall layout is the simplest of plans, but requires many steps and a lot of retracing of steps in meal preparation.

The ideal floor plan eases the cook's work and enables others to enjoy the kitchen's warmth and fragrance without getting in the way.

~~~~~~

 Answer the following questions.

1.1   What are the three major kitchen elements that comprise the work triangle?

a sink, a stove and a refrigerator.

1.2   How much work space should there be on each side of the sink?

two feet

1.3   How many feet should each side of the work triangle be? _four to seven feet_

1.4   Where should the sink be located in an ideal arrangement? _between stove and refrigerator_

1.5   Which kitchen layout is the most efficient? Why?

U-shaped, equipment and cabinets are grouped on three sides of the Kitchen with the sink in the middle of the U.

1.6   Describe the L-shaped kitchen layout.

Equipment and cabinets are in a L-shaped with sometimes a island.

LARGE KITCHEN EQUIPMENT

The first things that come to mind when we think about large kitchen equipment are the refrigerator, range, and sinks. However, there are other items to consider: freezers, dishwashers, compactors, cabinets, countertops, and flooring. We will consider all of these to some extent in this section.

The purpose of the refrigerator is to preserve nutrients in foods and to keep food cold, thus preventing spoilage. A properly operating refrigerator keeps food at a temperature of 38 to 42 degrees Fahrenheit. Almost all refrigerators have a separate compartment for freezing. Food should be kept at a temperature low enough for safety for a few weeks or months. Some freezers require periodic defrosting. Storage compartments, number, and adjustability of shelves, humidity drawers, meat storage compartments, location and range of temperature controls, ice-maker, defrost options, direction of door opening, and energy-saving devices will vary from model to model.

The purpose of the freezer is to store foods for a long period of time (six months to a year). The temperature is kept at below zero degrees Fahrenheit. It is important that foods be wrapped or packaged in airtight containers before storing. A freezer needs defrosting only about once a year or until the frost build-up is 1/2 to 1 inch thick.

The range is usually gas or electric. Gas units heat and cool quickly; the flame is visible and easy to control. Gas ranges have either **radiant** or **convection**/radiant ovens; lower ovens may be self-cleaning. Electric units provide low, even heat; they may have coil or smooth cook-tops, and radiant or convection/radiant ovens. The difference between a radiant and a convection oven is that the convection oven circulates hot air around the oven cavity; more energy-efficient than radiant ovens, they cut cooking time by 30 percent and use reduced temperatures. Electric cook-tops with ceramic glass over the coils heat and cool slowly, retaining heat up to an hour after shutoff. They need flat bottom pans for cooking and special products and care for cleaning. The last option available for ovens is the microwave. Foods cook quickly with high-frequency microwaves but seldom brown.

The sink is used for washing food during its preparation, for washing dishes, and for general cleaning. Commercially available sinks have one, two or three bowls with or without attached drain boards. They are generally made of stainless steel, enameled cast iron, enameled steel or porcelain on steel. A garbage disposal may be part of the sink. Most are electric and cut garbage into little pieces that can be washed through the drain into the sewer. This keeps bug-attracting food scraps out of the trash can.

The automatic dishwasher, whether portable or built-in, is a convenience that has become a part of almost every home. Since there are so many varieties and options available, be sure to follow the manufacturer's instructions for use and cleaning. Be sure to use special automatic dishwasher detergent only.

Trash compactors reduce bulky trash such as cartons, cans, and bottles to a fourth of the original size. New laws on recycling affect virtually everyone. A common problem is where to put recyclable items before they are collected or taken to the recycling center. Many kitchens feature special compartments or bins for recyclable items, but extra trash cans or boxes lined with plastic can work as well.

Cabinets determine a kitchen's "personality." The wide range of available styles and sizes allows you great freedom for creativity. Make sure that the space provided is divided so that you can use it all and there is no wasted space. Turntables in the corner units are a good way to utilize otherwise wasted space.

The vast array of kitchen flooring materials provides a palette that would please any artist. But beyond **aesthetic** consideration, it is important to consider how durable it is, how easy it is to keep clean and shiny, how comfortable it is to walk or stand on and how noisy it is.

The last of the large kitchen equipment we will consider is the countertop. Once again, the selection is expansive both in color and in materials used. Materials range from plastics to wood to ceramic, marble or tile. The color ranges are infinite.

Answer the following questions.

1.7   What is the purpose of the refrigerator? _to Kept foodcold_

1.8   How long can you store foods in the freezer? _to Kept food cold for long periods of time_

1.9   List the two types of ranges. a. _gas_   b. _Electric_

1.10   How does a convection oven differ from a radiant oven? _Convection cooks faster and turns off right a way, radiant, takes long time to cook and take long time to off._

1.11   What is a garbage disposal? _cuts up food_

1.12   What is an advantage of having a garbage disposal in your home? _Kepts bugs out of your trash can._

1.13   What determines the "personality" of the kitchen? _Cabinets, flooring, countertop,_

1.14   What are some considerations to address when selecting kitchen flooring? _how durable it is, how easy to clean, how comfortable it is._

SMALL KITCHEN APPLIANCES

There are many small appliances that you may use as often as your major appliances. These may include toasters, toaster ovens, mixers, bread makers, can openers, coffee makers, food processors, electric skillets, electric slow cookers with deep fryers, electric knives, electric crock pots, and waffle irons. Most counter-top appliances come with cleaning and care instructions from the manufacturer; follow these instructions carefully. One of the most important instructions to look for is to note whether an appliance is **immersible**; that is, can the appliance be submerged in water.

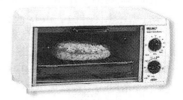

Toaster Oven: A portable electrical appliance that can function as an oven or a toaster.

Toaster: An electric appliance that will warm or brown bread, waffles, English muffins, etc.

Hand-held electric mixer: Compact in size and easy to use. An electric mixer allows you to whip egg whites or cream in seconds. Depending on the power of the motor, some will even mix cake batter and cookie dough.

Bread Machine: a typical bread machine has a mixing/rising/baking compartment and a control panel for setting the cycle, delay start timer, and bread color.

Stand mixer: Bulkier than a hand-held mixer, but will quickly mix cake batter and bread dough. More powerful motor than hand-held mixer and allows freedom of your hands.

Electric grinders: These will quickly produce freshly ground coffee, spices, and peppercorns. They are also useful for grinding nuts.

Electric can opener: electric appliance used to open cans. Some have knife sharpeners in the back.

Electric skillet: by placing food directly into the pan you can fry, slow cook, and bake. It is used just like an extra burner to your stove.

Coffee makers: can be percolator or drip types. The most popular is the drip type. Many come with timers that can be set so coffee is ready when you wake up in the morning.

Blenders: used to puree soups, sauces, and other liquids. They cannot be used for solids alone.

Waffle iron: an electric appliance that comes with reversible plates so it can be used to make pancakes as well as waffles. There are also waffle irons available for making Belgian waffles only.

Electric crock pot: used for slow cooking, stews and sauces. The lining is made of crockery to help keep foods from burning while cooking slowly. Some come with a removable crock pot so that you can use the heating pot as a frying pan for deep frying foods such as chicken, French fries or onion rings.

Although the above list of electric appliances helps to relieve some of the hard work involved in cooking for your family, not all of them are required for you to accomplish that task. For example, bread was baked, coffee was brewed, and cans were opened long before electric appliances were invented. The real key to providing a balanced and delicious meal is creativity and a willing heart.

Define the following words.

1.15   Immersible _____

1.16   Toaster _____

1.17   Blender _____

1.18   Crock pot _____

1.19   Waffle iron _____

Answer the following questions.

1.20   What are some advantages of a stand mixer over the hand-held mixer?_____

_____

1.21   What are the three basic steps in making bread?_____

_____

1.22   What small appliance can serve as an extra burner to your stove? _____

1.23   An electric grinder is used mostly for producing freshly ground_____ .

1.24   What are two types of coffee makers? _____

UTENSILS

Kitchen utensils cover a wide spectrum of useful items. For the sake of clarity, the utensils are divided into five categories: measuring equipment, ovenware, pots and pans, cutlery and kitchen tools, and conveniences.

Measuring Equipment

A clear glass one-cup or two-cup measuring cup with a spout and clearly marked calibrations is useful for measuring liquids.

Measuring cups are used for measuring dry ingredients such as flour, sugar, cornmeal, dried beans, and rice. You should have at least one set of 1/8 cup, 1/4 cup, 1/3 cup, 1/2 cup, and 1 cup.

Measuring spoons range from 1/4 teaspoon to 1 tablespoon; some sets contain 1/8 teaspoon and a 3/4 teaspoon. Use spoons to measure small amounts of liquids and dry ingredients.

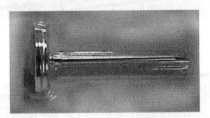

A meat thermometer is used to measure the internal temperature of meat or poultry during cooking.

Answer the following questions.

1.25 Measuring cups are used for measuring _____ such as _____

_____ .

1.26 What do you use to measure liquids? _____

1.27 Measuring spoons are used to measure small amounts of _____ and _____ .

1.28 A meat thermometer is used to measure the _____ temperature of meat or poultry during cooking.

OVENWARE

Cooking in an oven requires sturdy pans and dishes that conduct and retain heat efficiently. For added convenience, choose baking dishes that are attractive and can be used as serving dishes as well.

Roasting pans are made of heavy stainless steel or aluminum. It is best to have two sizes if possible. Roasting in a pan that is too large will cause juices to evaporate and burn; if the pan is too small it will be difficult to baste the meat or poultry properly.

Cake pans for baking cakes come in a variety of sizes and styles: 8-inch or 9-inch square pan, 8- or 9-inch round pan, 9x13-inch rectangular pan, angel food cake pan, and a bundt cake pan. An angel food cake pan has a funnel in the center for better baking and cooling. A bundt cake is similar, except it usually has fluted sides. There are many specialty cake pans of various shapes such as animals, T-shirts, shoes, cartoon characters, and numbers, that are fun to use.

Muffin pan for baking muffins and cupcakes.

Baking sheets for cookies and meringue.

Loaf pans for baking breads, cooking meatloaf, and baking loaf cakes.

Pie pans can be made of metal or glass and are usually 8 inches or 9 inches in diameter. A deep dish pie pan is used for deep dish apple or other fruit pies.

Answer the following questions.

1.29   What two qualities should you look for in ovenware? _____

1.30   Why is it bad to roast in a pan that is too large? _____

1.31   What is the use for a loaf pan? _____

1.32   List two uses for a muffin pan. _____

1.33   What are two materials used in making pie pans? _____

POTS AND PANS

Pans used on top of the stove must be heavy enough to sit securely on the burner without tipping, yet not too heavy to lift. A heavy base is important for gentle, even heat distribution. Pots and pans should have tight-fitting lids and handles that stay cool to the touch. Oven-proof handles make your pans more versatile.

A saucepan is a metal cooking pan of moderate depth, usually having a long handle and a tight-fitting lid. You will need to have a one-quart, a two-quart, and a three-quart saucepan.

A frying pan or skillet is a shallow, long-handled saucepan used for frying foods. It is good to have at least two; one 8-inch and one 12-inch. It is best if they have lids so the food can be covered and allowed to simmer. A non-stick skillet is good to have for making food items such as pancakes, French toast and grilled cheese sandwiches.

A large kettle or soup pot is also known as a stock pot. It should have a lid to keep in the nutrients and flavor. It is great for boiling lobster and cooking pasta as well as soups.

A double boiler is great for keeping things warm without overcooking them. It can also be used to melt caramels or chocolates.

A collapsible metal steamer that fits inside one of your larger saucepans is a convenient but not essential way to make rice and crispy vegetables.

Answer the following questions.

1.34   What qualities do you look for in a good pan?_____

_____

1.35   What is the use of a skillet?_____

1.36   What is the purpose of using the lids on pots and pans?_____

1.37   What pan do you use if you want to keep foods warm without overcooking them?

_____

CUTLERY AND CHOPPING

A set of sturdy, well-made knives that are kept sharp is essential for efficient food preparation. Knives are the most frequently used items in the kitchen. Different kinds of foods and different kinds of food cutting jobs require different lengths and shapes of blades. A basic set should include a 3-inch paring knife, a 5- or 6-inch utility knife, an 8- or 9-inch steak and poultry knife, a 9-inch roast slicer, an 8- or 10-inch French cook's or chef's knife and a serrated-edge bread, and cake knife.

chef's

roast

serrated

steak

utility

paring

The paring and utility knives are used in peeling and slicing most fruits and vegetables. Chopping, mincing, dicing, and cubing can be done with the chef's knife as well as the paring and utility knives. There are also specialty knives available such as a tomato knife which is like a utility or paring knife that has a serrated edge and a grapefruit knife that has double serrated edges and a curved tip for sectioning the grapefruit.

You judge the quality of a knife by the metal and the grind of the blade, the type of handle and the way the handle is attached to the blade. The two most widely used blades are the hollow ground edge which is straight and the scalloped serrated-edge blade. The blades should be made of stainless steel. Knife handles should be durable— resisting splitting or chipping—and dishwasher safe. The part of the blade extending into the handle is called the tang. It should extend in at least one-third the overall handle length.

For effective, efficient results, keep knives sharp by resetting the edge occasionally before using. This is done with a sharpening steel. Serrated-edge knives stay sharp for years and rarely need resetting.

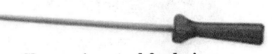

Sharpening steel for knives.

Remember, the kitchen knife is a piece of fine cutlery. There are other utensils and tools for other jobs. To save their fine edges and prevent accidents, use knives only for the purposes for which they are intended.

When the job is done and the knives are clean and dry, they should be stored separately so that the cutting edges will not become dulled by striking against each other or against other utensils.

In addition to the knives, some cutlery sets include a 2-pronged carving fork. This is a useful item for holding meats and poultry in place while cutting.

Another important item for the kitchen is the cutting board. If at all possible you should have two cutting boards; one for only meats and poultry and another for only breads and vegetables.

 Answer the following questions.

1.38   List the six knives that make up a good basic set of cutlery. _____

_____

1.39   How does a tomato knife differ from a regular utility knife? _____

1.40   Describe a grapefruit knife. _____

13

1.41 How do you judge the quality of a knife?_____

_____

1.42 A knife blade should be made of what type of metal?_____

1.43 Define *tang*. _____

Listed below are the many kitchen tools and conveniences that make working in the kitchen so much easier. Be sure you can recognize, name and give the use of each.

Apple corer:
for removing the seeds and core of the apple.

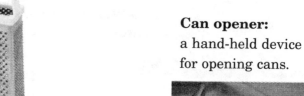

Box grater:
with 3 or 4 different cutting surfaces, from coarse to fine, for grating cheese, garlic, and nutmeg.

Can opener:
a hand-held device for opening cans.

Candy thermometer

Funnel:
for pouring liquids into containers with small openings.

Colander:
with legs, or a base, so it is free-standing.

Flour sifter:
for sifting and mixing dry ingredients together.

Juice squeezer:
preferably with a guard to catch the seeds.

Kitchen scissors:
made from stainless steel for easy cleaning.

Large spatula:
for turning and lifting
large food items.

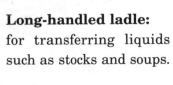

Long-handled ladle:
for transferring liquids
such as stocks and soups.

Grapefruit knife

Rolling pin:
long and heavy for
rolling pastry.

Narrow spatula:
with a 10-inch blade for
turning and lifting food.

Paper towel dispenser

Mortar and pestle:
ideal for grinding
herbs.

Pastry cutters:
plain and fluted, for cookies,
biscuits and tartlets.

Pastry or basting brushes:
for glazing pastry, greasing
cake pans, and brushing
meats with marinades.

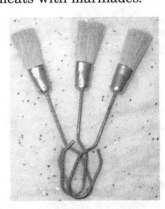

Pastry blender:
for blending flour and shortening together.

Vegetable peeler:
for peeling the skin off
of vegetables and fruit.

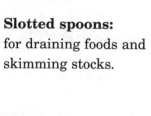

Sieve:
for straining liquids.

Wooden spoons:
in varying sizes.

Rubber spatulas:
for scraping bowls
clean.

Vegetable brush:
for cleaning dirt from vegetables.

Wire whisk:
for whipping eggs,
cream, and sauces.

Potato masher

Strainer:
rigid metal mesh for sifting dry
ingredients; flexible nylon for
straining sauces and purees.

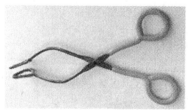

Tongs:
for turning meat while cooking
without piercing it.

16

Mixing bowls:
Set of 3 or 4 in varying sizes; stainless steel or glass.

Wire rack:
for cooling cakes, cookies, and breads.

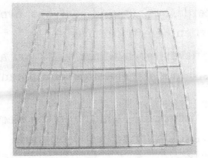

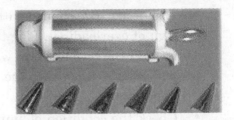

Small cake decorating set:
for piping whipped cream and icing on cakes and desserts, and shaping meringue and puff pastry.

 Complete the following activity.

1.44 Go into your kitchen and find as many of the kitchen tools listed in this section as you can. Be sure you can identify them by name. Review the use of each item.

 Adult Check _____

Initial   Date

KITCHEN SAFETY

Now that you are acquainted with the kitchen, it should be easy for you to understand with so many electrical appliances and kitchen tools the importance for kitchen safety. Kitchens are no longer used for food preparation alone, but also function as dining, entertainment, hobby, and office areas as well. Therefore, ensuring kitchen safety is even more important.

- Reduce the fire potential by storing flammable items away from heat. Clean the entire cooking area frequently; grease buildup can be dangerous, yet it often goes unnoticed.

- Install a smoke detector between the kitchen and living areas and keep a fire extinguisher handy.

- If fire breaks out on a cooktop, cover the flames with a pot lid, apply baking soda or salt, or use the extinguisher. **Never** douse a grease fire with water and do not attempt to move a flaming pan. To smother a fire in an oven, turn off the heat and keep the oven door closed.

Have a fire extinguisher handy.

- Know the location of your main gas shutoff valve and how to operate it.

- Sparks can ignite gas—don't turn on electric switches, appliances or other ignition sources if you suspect a leak.

17

- Use properly grounded outlets with circuit breakers. Don't overload your circuits (hot plugs are a sign of overloading). Plug the cord into the appliance first, then into the wall outlet. Always disconnect the cord from the wall outlet before removing it from the appliance—otherwise a "hot" plug will be exposed. Grasp the plug rather than the cord when removing the cord from the outlet or appliance.

- Check the condition of appliance cords, outlets, and switches; avoid using extension cords. Know where and how to turn off your kitchen's electrical circuits.

- Keep appliances away from water; never touch water while you are using them. Dry your hands thoroughly before connecting or disconnecting electrical equipment. Always unplug appliances for cleaning and repairs.

- Never use a metal or wooden spoon, a fork or a spatula in the electric-mixer bowl while it is operating. Instead use a rubber scraper. Avoid getting batter or liquid into the mechanism of an electric mixer.

- Keep forks out of the electric toaster. Avoid shaking the toaster upside down to remove crumbs. Instead, empty the crumb tray.

- Kitchens invite exploration by children, so be prepared. Lock up chemicals and don't store harmful substances in empty food containers.

- Block electric outlets with safety plugs. Buy appliances with controls out of the reach of children. Keep knives and small appliances out of children's reach. Never let the cord dangle. It may cause the appliance to be pulled off the working area.

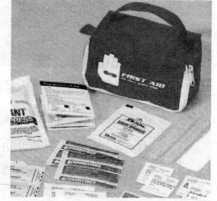
Keep a first aid kit handy.

- Keep a first aid kit in the kitchen for quick treatment of burns and cuts.

Answer the following questions.

1.45 How do you put out a fire on the cooktop? *you put a panlid on the pan and apply baking soda or salt.*

1.46 How do you smother a fire in the oven? *turn off heat and kept the door close,*

1.47 Which do you unplug first, the plug from the outlet or the plug from the appliance? *plug from the outlet.*

1.48 What is the best way to remove crumbs from the toaster? *remove the crumb tray.*

1.49 What are two safety tips concerning small children? *lock up chemicals, put safety plugs on outlet.*

Review the material in this section in preparation for the Self Test. The Self Test will check your mastery of this particular section. The items missed on this Self Test will indicate specific areas where restudy is needed for mastery.

SELF TEST 1

Answer *true* **or** *false* (each answer, 2 points).

1.01 _____true_____ There should be 3–6 feet on each side of the work triangle in a kitchen layout.

1.02 _____true_____ The U-shaped kitchen layout is the most efficient.

1.03 _____true_____ You can store food in the freezer for 6 months to a year.

1.04 _____true_____ The flooring determines the "personality" of the kitchen.

1.05 _____false_____ A skillet is used to fry foods.

1.06 _____true_____ Lids should be used on pots and pans to keep in nutrients and flavor.

1.07 _____true_____ The quality of a knife is judged by its length and sharpness.

1.08 _____false_____ Put out a grease fire with water.

1.09 _____true_____ Unplug an electrical cord from the wall outlet before you unplug it from the appliance.

1.010 _____true_____ Always use a rubber scraper in the bowl of an electric mixer if you are going to scrape while the mixer is operating.

Answer the following questions (each answer, 3 points).

1.011 The three major work stations that comprise the work triangle are the sink, stove, and _____refrigerator_____ .

1.012 Why is it bad to roast in a pan that is too big? _because the liquides can seperate and bord_

1.013 The purpose of the refrigerator is to preserve __nutrients__ and to keep food cold to prevent spoilage.

1.014 The two types of ranges are gas and __electricity__ .

1.015 The three basic steps in making bread are mixing, __resting__ , and baking.

1.016 A meat thermometer is used to measure the ____Heat____ temperature of meat or poultry during cooking.

1.017 Name one safety tip concerning small children in the kitchen. _cover outlets with safety plugs._

19

Identify the following items (each answer, 2 points).

1.018 <u>toaster oven</u>

1.019 <u>standing mixer</u>

1.020 <u>coffee maker</u>

1.021 <u>wisk</u>

dry
1.022 <u>measuring cups</u>

1.023 <u>measuring spoon</u>

glass
1.024 <u>measuring cups</u>

1.025 <u>cake pans</u>

1.026 <u>pie pan</u>

(1.027) <u>glass pot</u>

1.028 <u>pot</u>

1.029 <u>Grapefuite knif</u>

20

1.030 <u>large spatula</u> 1.031 <u>rolling pin</u> 1.032 <u>derainer</u>

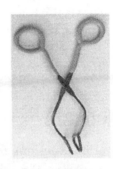

1.033 <u>potato masher</u> 1.034 <u>tongs</u> 1.035 <u>cooling rake</u>

1.036 <u>peeler</u>

Describe the L-shaped kitchen layout using either words or pictures (3 points).

1.037 _____

_____

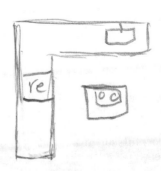

66 / 82

Score — <u>86%</u>

Adult Check — <u>Mom 10-7-16</u>

Initial   Date

21

II. RECIPES

What is a recipe? What makes a recipe good? Is there a basic formula for writing a recipe? Of course, the answer to these questions and others will be addressed in this LIFEPAC section. Learning basic terms, abbreviations, equivalents, and measurements are all essential parts of understanding recipes. There is a lot to consider, so let's get going.

SECTION OBJECTIVES

Review these objectives. When you have completed this section, you should be able to:

4. Identify what to look for in a good recipe and how to read a recipe.
5. Identify cooking terms, abbreviations, equivalents, and measurements found in recipes.

WHAT TO LOOK FOR IN A GOOD RECIPE

The dictionary defines recipe as "a set of instructions for making or preparing something, especially a food dish." In order for a recipe to be a good recipe the instructions must be complete and easily understood. What to look for in a good recipe and the steps for writing a good recipe are listed below.

- List *ingredients* in the order of their use.
- Give exact *measurements* of all ingredients.
- Include simple, step-by-step *directions* listed in the order in which they are to be done.
- Give the exact cooking *time*.
- Give the exact cooking *temperature*.
- Tell the size of the cooking *utensil* to use.
- Give the number and size of *servings* the recipe will make.
- It should be a *tested* recipe.

ingredients   servings

Grandma's Chocolate Chip Cookies

Makes about 4 dozen cookies

measurements

3/4	cup granulated sugar
3/4	cup packed brown sugar
1	cup margarine
1	large egg
2 1/4	cups all purpose flour
1	teaspoon baking soda
1/2	teaspoon salt
1	cup coarsely chopped nuts
1	package (12 ounces) semisweet chocolate chips (2 cups)

temperature

1. Heat oven to **375 degrees**
2. Mix sugars, margarine, and egg in large bowl. Stir in flour, baking soda, and salt (dough will be stiff). Stir in nuts and chocolate chips.

directions

3. Drop dough by rounded tablespoonfuls about 2 inches apart onto ungreased cookie sheet.

time

4. Bake **8 to 10 minutes** or until light brown (centers will be soft) Cool slightly, remove from cookie sheet. Cool on wire

Complete the following activity:

2.1 Review the steps for writing a good recipe. Find a recipe for chocolate chip cookies in three different cookbooks. Compare how the recipes were written and decide which recipe follows best the steps for a good recipe. Why did you select this recipe? _____

_____

Adult Check _____

                                                          Initial   Date

RECIPE INGREDIENTS

Now that you have a better understanding of what a good recipe includes, we will focus our attention on some of the particulars of recipes: ingredients, measurements of those ingredients and basic terms used in recipes.

There are seven basic groups in which ingredients can be placed: eggs, sweetener, flour, fats and oils, leavening agent, liquid, and seasoning or flavoring. Each of these seven groups has specific characteristics that help them do specific jobs.

1. *Eggs* as an ingredient in a variety of recipes add nutrients as well as richness, flavor, texture, thickening and/or **leavening**. Eggs also help form a stronger framework. For example, a cake made without eggs will have a tendency to be more crumbly.

2. *Sweetener* gives the recipe sweetness and tenderness. It also aids in browning. Sugar, of course, is the most common sweetener. It comes in three forms: granulated white sugar, brown sugar, and powdered sugar. Corn syrup is a clear, thick liquid made from corn sugar mixed with acid. It's one sweetener that doesn't crystallize and is especially good for pecan pie, frosting, and candy making.

3. *Flour* is the primary ingredient in breads, cakes, cookies, and quick breads. It thickens the mixture and holds ingredients together. Listed below are several different types of flour and their primary uses.

- All-purpose flour is used for all sorts of baking and is available both bleached and unbleached.

- Bread flour is the best choice for bread machines and yeast breads. For other baking, bread flour can make some recipes too tough.

- Cake flour results in tender, fine-textured cakes but is not recommended to substitute for all-purpose or bread flours.

- Quick-mix flour is meant for making gravies and sauces or to thicken main dishes.

- Rye flour is usually combined with wheat flour to increase the dough's **gluten**-forming capabilities.

- Self-rising flour is used for light and fluffy biscuits and tender cakes. Because it already contains leavening and salt, it should not be used as a substitute for others flours. The leavening and salt proportions would be inaccurate.

- Whole wheat flour gives a nutty flavor and dense texture to breads and other baked goods. Breads made with whole wheat flour rise less than those made with other types of flour.

You should become familiar with these because it can make a difference to the success or failure of a recipe, depending on the type of flour that is used.

4. *Fats and oils* add richness and flavor to food, aid in browning, help bind ingredients together, **tenderize** baked goods, and are used for frying. There are many types of fats and oils; they each have different cooking and baking characteristics. Be sure to use exactly what the recipe calls for so that you won't be disappointed in the results. For example, **lard** is softer and richer than butter or margarine and makes very tender, flaky biscuits and pastry. Reduced-calorie or low-fat butter or margarine and vegetable spreads contain less fat and more water and air and are not suitable for baking or making candies. Oils for cooking are low in saturated fats and contain no cholesterol. These liquid fats are delicate to bland in flavor and are created to withstand high-temperature cooking and long storage.

5. *Leavening agents* make batters and dough rise and lighten. Some of the most used are baking powder, baking soda and **yeast**. Yeast is the leavening agent whose **fermentation** is the essence of yeast bread. The combination of warmth, sugar, and liquid causes yeast to release carbon dioxide bubbles that cause the dough to rise. Always use yeast before the expiration date.

6. *Liquids* give moisture for blending the dry ingredients. They also start the leavening action. Milk products and water are the two most often used liquids in recipes.

7. *Seasoning or flavoring* adds interest to your recipes. They come in the form of spices, chocolates, herbs, peppers and chilies, sauces and sweeteners.

Answer the following questions.

2.2   What do eggs do as an ingredient in recipes? _____

_____

2.3   What are the three types of sugar? _____

2.4   What kind of sweetener does not crystallize? _____

2.5   Why can't bread flour be substituted for all-purpose flour in most recipes? _____

_____

2.6   What does self-rising flour contain that other flours do not?_____

2.7   Why is it important to use the correct type of fat or oil? Give an example. _____

_____

24

2.8   Explain how yeast works as a leavening agent._____

_____

2.9   What are the two most used liquids in recipes?_____

2.10   Seasoning or flavoring adds _____ to your recipe.

....

Not only is it important to know what ingredients are found in recipes and to understand what their role is in the overall success of the recipe, but it is extremely important to know how to measure these ingredients accurately. Too much or too little of an ingredient can ruin the final outcome of your recipe. Here are some tips for measuring ingredients with accuracy and ease.

- For flour, baking mix, and sugar, spoon the ingredient lightly into a dry measuring cup, then level with a straight-edged spatula or knife. Sift powdered sugar only if it is lumpy.

- For cereal and dry bread crumbs, pour into dry measuring cup. Level with a straight-edged spatula or knife.

- For shredded cheese, chopped nuts, coconut, and soft bread crumbs, spoon into dry measuring cup and pack down lightly.

- For solid fats and brown sugar, spoon into dry measuring cup and pack down firmly with spatula and spoon. If you use a metal measuring cup for the solid fat, warming it slightly will allow the ingredient to be removed easier.

- For very small amounts of thin liquids, pour into spoon until full.

- For very small amounts of dry ingredients, pour or scoop into spoon until full, then level with a straight-edged spatula or knife.

- For an accurate measure of liquids, pour the ingredient into a glass measuring cup. Always read the measurement at eye level while the cup is on a flat surface.

- To measure sticky liquids such as honey, molasses, and corn syrup, spray a little oil into the liquid measuring cup first so the liquid will be easier to remove.

Measure your ingredients accurately.

....

There are equivalent measurements that are used in recipes that would be helpful for you to be familiar with. The following table gives the most common equivalent measures.

Measurement:	Equivalent:
Dash	about 1/8 tsp
3 teaspoons	1 tablespoon
4 tablespoon	1/4 cup
5 tablespoon + 1 teaspoon	1/3 cup
8 tablespoons	1/2 cup

16 tablespoons	1 cup
1 cup	8 fluid ounces
2 cups	1 pint
4 cups (2 pints)	1 quart
4 quarts	1 gallon (liquid)
8 quarts	1 peck (dry)
16 ounces	1 pound

Abbreviations Used in Recipes.

c	cup
° (or dg)	degree
doz	dozen
fg	few grains
gal	gallon
hr	hour
″ (or in.)	inch
min	minute
oz	ounce
pkg	package
pt	pint
lb (or #)	pound
qt	quart
sec	second
Tbsp (or T)	tablespoon
tsp (or t)	teaspoon

Answer *true* or *false*.

2.11 _____ You should always sift powdered sugar.

2.12 _____ When measuring dry ingredients, you should level with a knife or straight-edge spatula.

2.13 _____ Cheese and brown sugar should be packed down firmly for an accurate measurement.

2.14 _____ There are two teaspoons in a tablespoon.

2.15 _____ There are eight quarts in one peck.

Answer the following questions with short answers.

2.16 How do you read liquid measurements accurately? _____

_____

2.17 There are _____ ounces in one pound.

There are many terms associated with recipes. These terms are divided into two categories: mixing terms and cooking terms. Learn these terms and their definitions.

Mixing Terms

Beat: Combine ingredients vigorously with spoon, fork, wire whisk, hand beater or electric mixer until smooth and uniform.

Blend: Mix two or more ingredients.

Cream: Make a mixture soft and smooth by rubbing or beating it with a spoon, fork, wooden paddle, rotary beater or electric mixer.

Cut in: Distribute shortening or solid fat in dry ingredients by cutting with a pastry blender or crisscrossing two knives until the particles are at a desired size.

Fold: Mix ingredients together while preventing the loss of air by using two motions. First, cut straight down vertically through the mixture. Second, slide spatula across the bottom of the mixing bowl and up the side, turning the mixture over and over.

Getting ready to bake.

Mix: Combine ingredients, usually by stirring.

Process: Use either a food processor or a mini chopper to liquefy, blend, chop, grind or knead food.

Stir: Mix ingredients together with a circular motion, using a spoon or a fork.

Whip: Beat ingredients to add air and increase volume until ingredients are light and fluffy.

Cooking Terms

Bake: Cook in the oven by dry heat.

Baste: Spoon pan drippings, water or sauce over food while roasting it.

Batter: An uncooked mixture of flour, eggs, and liquid with other ingredients; thin enough to be spooned or poured (muffins, pancakes).

Blanch: Plunge food into boiling water for a brief time to preserve color, texture, and nutritional value or to remove skin.

Boil: Cook in boiling water or other liquid that is bubbling and steaming.

Braise: Cook in a small amount of water in a covered container.

Broil: Cook directly under or over the source of heat.

Brown: Bake, fry, or toast a food until the surface is brown.

Caramelize: Melt sugar slowly over low heat until it becomes a golden brown, caramel-flavored syrup.

Chill: Place in the refrigerator until it is cold.

Chop: Cut into small pieces.

Coat: Cover food evenly with crumbs or sauce.

Cool: Allow hot food to stand at room temperature for a specified amount of time.

Core: Remove the center of a fruit.

Crisp-tender: Doneness description of vegetables cooked until they retain some of the crisp texture of the raw food.

Dash: Less than 1/8 teaspoon of an ingredient.

Debone: Remove the bones from fish, poultry or meat.

Dice: Cut into very small cubes (less than 1/2 inch).

Dissolve: Stir a dry ingredient into a liquid ingredient until the dry ingredient disappears.

Dot: Scatter small bits of a substance, usually margarine, on top of a food.

Dough: Mixture of flour and liquid with other ingredients; it is stiff but pliable.

Drain: Pour off liquid by putting the food into a strainer or colander that has been set in the sink.

Flute: Squeeze pastry edge with fingers to make a finished, ornamental edge.

Fry: Cook in hot fat. The words "panfry" and "sauté" mean to cook in just enough fat to cover the bottom of the pan. "Deep fry" or "french fry" means to cook in enough fat to cover food being fried.

Glaze: Coat a food with syrup or jelly and then heat or chill it.

Grate: Rub a hard-textured food against the small rough, sharp-edged holes of a grater, reducing them to tiny particles.

Grease: Rub the inside surface of a pan with shortening, using a pastry brush, waxed paper or paper towel, to prevent food from sticking during baking.

Julienne: Cut into thin, match-like strips using knife or food processor.

Knead: Press dough with the palms of the hands, turning the dough slightly as you push it.

Marinate: Allow food to stand in a savory liquid before cooking.

Melt: Change a solid food into a liquid by heating it.

Mince: Cut food into very fine pieces, smaller than chopped food.

Mold: Place a food in a dish or mold until it congeals or hardens.

Pare / Peel: Cut off the outer covering.

Poach: To cook in simmering liquid just below the boiling point.

Preheat: Heat an oven to the desired temperature before putting in the food.

Roast: Cook meat in uncovered, shallow pan in an oven.

Scald: Heat liquid to just below the boiling point. Tiny bubbles will form at the edge. A thin skin will form on the top of milk.

Score: Cut surface of food about 1/4 inch deep, using a knife.

Sift: Put dry ingredients through a sieve.

Simmer: Cook in liquid on range top, just below the boiling point.

Steam: Cook food by placing on a rack or special steamer basket over a small amount of boiling or simmering water in a covered pan.

Stew: Cook slowly in a small amount of liquid for a long time.

Strain: Pour mixture or liquid through a fine sieve or strainer to remove large particles.

Toss: Tumble ingredients lightly with a lifting motion, such as a salad with greens.

Complete the following activities.

2.18   Find the correct items in the word search below. Then, match the terms with their correct definition.

```
B E A T X L S C P
L R W I N F U T B
E K M C J T I D L
N U G R I S S P R
D X B N X T S O M
H E I L V I E C K
T S M A E R C O L
S A T I O F O L D
U S H T S R R B O
C R E W H I P E F
```

a.   _____   Mix two or more ingredients.

b.   _____   Mix ingredients together while preventing the loss of air.

c.   _____   Mix ingredients together with a circular motion, using a spoon or fork.

d.   _____   Make a mixture soft and smooth by rubbing or beating it with a spoon.

e.   _____   Liquefy, blend, chop, grind, or knead food.

f.   _____   Beat ingredients to add air and increase volume.

g.   _____   Distribute solid fat in dry ingredients by cutting with a pastry blender.

h.   _____   Combine ingredients, usually by stirring.

2.19   Unscramble the words and match to the definitions.

a.   asrieb   _____   f.   ovdissle   _____

b.   clnabh   _____   g.   tephare   _____

c.   letm   _____   h.   tufel   _____

d.   lobir   _____   i.   unilneje   _____

e.   loco   _____   j.   wrobn   _____

1.   _____   Cook directly under or over the source of heat.

2.   _____   Squeeze pastry edge with fingers to make a finished, ornamental edge.

3.   _____   Plunge food into boiling water for a brief time to remove skin.

4.   _____   Stir a dry ingredient into a liquid ingredient until the dry ingredient disappears.

5.   _____   Heat oven to desired temperature before putting in the food.

6.   _____   Change a solid food into a liquid by heating it.

7.   _____   Cut into thin, match-like strips with a knife.

8.   _____   Allow hot food to stand at room temperature for a specified amount of time.

9.   _____   Bake, fry or toast a food until the surface is brown.

10.   _____   Cook in a small amount of water in a covered container.

Complete the crossword puzzle of basic cooking terms.

2.20

Across: 1. Spoon pan drippings, water or sauce over food while roasting it.

4. Cut food into very fine pieces, smaller than chopped food.

9. Allow food to stand in a savory liquid before cooking.

10. Tumble ingredients lightly with a lifting motion, such as a salad with greens.

11. Mixture of flour and liquid with other ingredients; it is stiff, but pliable.

13. Coat a food with syrup or jelly and then heat or chill it.

15. Heat liquid to just below the boiling point.

Down: 1. An uncooked mixture of flour, eggs, and liquid with other ingredients.

2. Pour mixture or liquid through a fine sieve to remove large particles.

3. Cook liquid on range top, just below the boiling point.

5. Melt sugar slowly over low heat until it becomes a golden brown.

6. Cook meat in uncovered, shallow pan in an oven.

7. Cook slowly in a small amount of liquid for a long time.

8. Press dough with the palms of the hands, turning the dough slightly as you push it.

12. Rub the inside surface of a pan with shortening.

14. Cook food by placing it in a special basket over a small amount of boiling water in a covered pan.

Review the material in this section in preparation for the Self Test. The Self Test will check your mastery of this particular section. The items missed on this Self Test will indicate specific areas where restudy is needed for mastery.

SELF TEST 2

List the steps for writing a good recipe (each answer, 2 points).

2.01 _____

2.02 _____

2.03 _____

2.04 _____

2.05 _____

2.06 _____

2.07 _____

2.08 _____

Matching (each answer, 2 points).

2.09 _____ primary ingredient in breads, cakes, and cookies.

2.010 _____ starts the leavening action.

2.011 _____ adds nutrients and helps form a stronger framework.

2.012 _____ adds richness and flavor to food, aids in browning, and used for frying.

2.013 _____ makes batters and dough rise and lighten.

2.014 _____ adds interest to your recipes.

2.015 _____ gives recipe sweetness and tenderness; aids in browning.

a. eggs

b. sweetener

c. flour

d. fats and oils

e. leavening agent

f. liquid

g. seasoning and flavoring

Answer the following questions (each answer, 3 points).

2.016 What is the correct way to measure flour and sugar? _____

_____

2.017 What is the correct way to measure brown sugar? _____

_____

2.018 What is the correct way to measure small amounts of a thin liquid? _____

_____

2.019 What is the correct way to measure larger amounts of liquid? _____

_____

31

Fill the blank with the correct equivalent (each answer, 2 points).

2.020 3 teaspoons equal _____ tablespoon(s)

2.021 8 tablespoons equal _____ cup(s)

2.022 1 cup equals _____ fluid ounce(s)

2.023 8 quarts equal _____ peck(s)

2.024 16 ounces equal _____ pound(s)

Matching (each answer, 2 points).

2.025 _____ Mix ingredients together preventing the loss of air.

2.026 _____ Cook in hot fat.

2.027 _____ Pour mixture or liquid through a fine sieve to remove large particles.

2.028 _____ Spoon pan drippings, water, or sauce over food while roasting it.

2.029 _____ Beat ingredients to add air and increase volume.

2.030 _____ Tumble ingredients lightly with a lifting motions, such as a salad with greens.

2.031 _____ Make a mixture soft and smooth by rubbing or beating it.

2.032 _____ Cut food into very fine pieces, smaller than chopped food.

2.033 _____ Rub a hard-textured food against the small rough, sharp-edged holes of a grater, reducing them to tiny particles.

2.034 _____ Combine ingredients, usually by stirring.

a. baste

b. cream

c. fold

d. mix

e. whip

f. fry

g. grate

h. strain

i. toss

j. mince

Answer *true* **or** *false* (each answer, 2 points).

2.035 _____ The L-shaped kitchen layout is the most efficient.

2.036 _____ The toaster oven can function as an extra burner to your stove.

2.037 _____ The double boiler is a pan used to keep foods warm without overcooking them.

2.038 _____ A paring knife is used for peeling and slicing fruits and vegetables.

2.039 _____ A serrated-edge knife is used to slice bread and cake or section grapefruit.

66	
	82

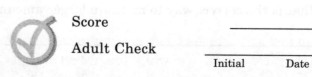

Score _____

Adult Check _____

Initial   Date

III. MEAL MANAGEMENT

In these times of rising food prices and high **inflation**, it is good to sharpen your shopping skills to help save those pennies, nickels, dimes, and dollars. This section will help you learn how to eat nutritionally and economically while staying within a set budget.

SECTION OBJECTIVES

Review these objectives. When you have completed this section, you should be able to:

6. Identify the different aspects of meal management.
7. Demonstrate skill in maintaining a food budget through careful buying strategies.
8. Compare and contrast different types of food stores.
9. Demonstrate supermarket etiquette.
10. Identify nutritional and economic values from reading food labels.
11. Gain an understanding of various methods of proper food storage.
12. Explain the importance of proper food storage.

FOOD BUDGET

Smart food shopping begins at home with careful attention to meal planning for nutritional value and a shopping list shaped to your family needs. Budget carefully and spend only what you can afford. It is important to the family's financial stability that you create a food budget and stick with it. If you must cut some food from your grocery list, make sure you cut the frills and not the necessities. Nutrients are the necessities. It is important to get all the nutrients your body needs to function from the food you eat.

The easiest way to make sure you are getting all these nutrients is to select from a variety of foods, including milk, meat, fruit, vegetables, and grain products. Cut costs by avoiding extras like cake, candy, soft drinks, and low-nutrient snacks which provide little more than calories.

Buying on impulse can increase your grocery bill. The items you buy on impulse are probably the items you need least. Planning is the key to avoid impulse buying. The following strategies apply to shopping for any number of people.

- Read the midweek and Sunday newspaper food ads. Include specials in your weekly menu. Stock up on sale items for future use (storage space permitting).

- Make a shopping list and stick to it. Plan your shopping list around carefully planned menus.

- Shop after eating. Hunger may tempt you to overbuy.

- Clip and save coupons. File and organize your coupons so they are easy to use while you are shopping. Check

A supermarket ad.

33

the expiration dates. Watch for special double and triple coupon days at stores. Avoid clipping coupons for things you don't need.

- Be cautious. A bargain is not always a bargain. Check the prices and signs. For example, two-for-one items are a savings only if you can use both items. Use coupons with common sense. Getting a few pennies off an overpriced item isn't much of a bargain. Before you buy, check the price of the generic or store brand of the product.

- Free samples of foods and drinks are given to shoppers to encourage them to purchase these items. Before you buy them, make sure you really want them and will use them.

- Shopping with family or friends can result in impulse buying as "their" selections jump into "your" cart. Saying "no" to their impulse selections may be hard at first, but it will help you stick to your budget.

- Use unit prices. Check the price per measure (per ounce, per pound, per quart, etc.) of products in different sizes or brands. The largest size is not always the best buy. Example: a 6-ounce can of tomato paste for 36 cents has a unit price of 6 cents per ounce. A 12-ounce can of tomato paste for 78 cents has a unit price of 6.5 cents per ounce. In this case the smaller can of tomato paste is the best bargain.

- Many large supermarkets tend to have their own brand of products. In most cases, these products do save money and usually are comparable with name brands in quality. Items such as noodles, tomato paste, fabric softener, and grape jelly are fine. For others, you may find you prefer name brands. Taste, trial, and test is the key. Read labels for nutritional value. It is wise to note here that store brands are not always less expensive than name brand products; you cannot use manufacturer's coupons to buy them.

- More money-saving ideas:

  - Buy fresh fruits and vegetables during their peak growing seasons.

  - Prepare foods yourself if you have the time. It's usually cheaper than buying a ready prepared item.

  - If the store runs out of a sale item, ask for a rain-check.

- Compare cost of fresh, dried, canned, and frozen foods. To determine the best buy, divide the price by the number of servings.

  - Fresh vs. Frozen:

    - It is easier by far to cook frozen vegetables. You are ensured that there are vegetables in the house if you store them in your freezer where they won't spoil. However, taste-wise, fresh is better.

    - Stay away from frozen entrees. They cost a lot, are loaded with salt and are often lacking in nutrition.

- Frozen orange juice concentrate is fine unless you are not a milk drinker; then calcium-enriched orange juice is available by the carton as well as in concentrate.

- Canned vs. Fresh

  - Fresh ingredients are more flavorful than canned products. The major exceptions are canned tuna, canned soups (which can be added to dishes to improve taste), and tomatoes for sauces, stews, soups, and casseroles.

Canned vs. fresh tomatoes.

- Buying meat and produce in bulk can save money only if you can use it all. Be willing to take extra time and effort to cut whole chicken and cook a lesser grade of meat slowly or don't buy it. Remember, a low grade of ground beef means more fat to drain off and less meat to eat.

  - Although there's a big difference in price, there is little difference in the amount of protein between chuck and sirloin cuts of meat.

  - Select cuts that give the most lean meat for the money. Avoid cuts with a large amount of gristle, bone, and fat.

  - Cuts of meat containing more fat are usually more tender. However, these are usually more expensive than leaner cuts. Therefore, buy meat with only enough fat to enhance the flavor.

  - Choose low-cost sources of protein like fish, chicken and turkey, liver and other organ meats, eggs, milk and other dairy products, legumes (dry beans, peas, lentils), and nuts.

- Check produce for soft or brown spots, mold or rot. Lettuce heads should be heavy and firm, fruits solid and flawless. Look at the bottom of the basket of blueberries, raspberries, strawberries; do you see any mold? Melons should smell sweet and you should be able to push the end in slightly. A slightly green banana will ripen at home at room temperature. Apples are ripe, once they are at the store.

- No matter what size you buy, eggs are an excellent and inexpensive source of protein. Make eggs a part of your main meals by serving omelets, quiche, and other egg dishes. Remember, if larger eggs are seven cents more than the next smaller size, the smaller size is probably the better buy.

- To cut costs, some manufacturers use imitation instead of natural ingredients in their cheeses. Some frozen pizzas, for example, are made with imitation cheese or meat. Unfortunately, many consumers are paying for—and think they are getting—natural ingredients. Read food packages for words like "imitation," "substitute" and "artificial." On dairy products, look for the "REAL" Seal. It tells you the food is a genuine dairy product—not an imitation.

- Read the labels.

Can you really cut food costs without cutting the foods you enjoy and need for good nutrition? YES, but as you can see, it takes time and effort. Grocery shopping may never be recreational...but it will be a lot more pleasant if you know you are getting the most for your food dollar.

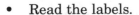

Answer *true* **or** *false*.

3.1 *false* To save money, cut out meat and dairy products.

3.2 *true* You get more protein for your money from a sirloin steak than you do from a chuck steak.

3.3 *true* The smallest size eggs are always the best buy.

3.4 *true* The economy size is always the best buy.

3.5 *true* Making a shopping list helps you spend less money in the store.

3.6 *false* It is best to shop on an empty stomach.

3.7 *true* Store brand food items are usually less expensive than name brands.

3.8 *false* You should collect and use all coupons you find.

3.9 *true* Frozen entrees cost a lot more and are loaded with salt.

3.10 *false* All frozen pizzas are made with real cheese.

3.11 *true* The best time to buy fresh fruits and vegetables is during their peak growing seasons.

SUPERMARKET SMARTS

We all have our favorite markets, of course, but loyalty to a chain can cost you. When another store offers an attractive special, it is acceptable to take advantage of the special.

There are different types of food stores, each has its advantages and disadvantages. Study the chart below to compare and contrast some of the different types of food stores.

Type of Food Store	Advantages	Disadvantages
Supermarket	Convenient. Wide selection of food. Variety in price ranges. Advertised specials. Longer store hours.	You can't find things quickly.
Warehouses	Low prices. Can buy in bulk.	Generally no customer service. Might have to buy large quantities. Limited amount of fresh produce. Less variety.
Co-op	Operated and owned by a group of people. Save money. Neighborhood involved.	Not a lot of variety. Buy in bulk.
Convenience Stores	Usually open 24 hours a day. Usually get fast service.	Usually higher priced. Selection is limited.

36

Specialty Stores	Get personal attention. Get fast service. Friendly and nice service	More expensive.
Thrift Store or Day-Old Store	Lower prices.	Limited selection. Must use sooner, shorter storage time.
Farmers' Market	Great fresh produce. Good prices. You can buy in bulk if you want.	Limited selection. Must use sooner, shorter storage time. Limited selection and hours.

No matter in which of the above food stores you choose to do your shopping, it is important for you to realize there are rules of behavior you should follow. The following do's and don'ts should help you be a good, polite, and efficient shopper.

- Don't run over peoples' heels with the grocery cart. Watch where you are going. It would be very embarrassing to run into another shopper or knock over a stack of canned goods.
- Don't leave your cart and go somewhere else.
- Be organized and know what you want. This will not only limit the number of trips through the same aisle, but will also save you time.
- Be gentle to the fruit.
- Be neat. If you pick something up, put it back where you got it. Leaving items that you decide you don't want in the wrong aisle is inconsiderate and can be wasteful if the food item is perishable.
- Don't let children run around. A loose child can be a danger not only to himself, but to others.
- Don't use the express lane if you have too many items.
- Have your coupons ready.
- Be kind to everyone in the store.
- When you are finished with your shopping cart, return it to the designated cart areas in the parking lot.

Answer the following questions.

3.12 Where can you go to get a carton of milk after midnight? _____

3.13 Where can you find a great bargain on bread? _____

3.14 What is the best food store to do your shopping if you are buying a week's groceries for a family of four? _____

3.15 Where do you go if you are looking for fresh lobster and money is no object? _____

3.16 Where can you find fresh corn on the cob at a good price? _____

3.17 Which type of store do you shop in if you are buying large amounts of food for a banquet? _____

_____

3.18 Why should you observe rules of behavior when shopping? _____

READING LABELS

Many packaged items contain combinations of foods or ingredients. Everything in the package listed in the ingredient line must be in a designated order: the first item is the most plentiful by percentage weight and the list continues in diminishing order down to the smallest quantity.

For example:

Ingredients: water, potatoes, carrots, peas, beef, onions, spices

Ingredients: beef, water, potatoes, carrots, onions, peas, spices

Answer the following questions. Use the above sample cans of stew to find the answers.

3.19 Which can of stew contains the most beef? _____

Name two ways you can know this. a. _____ and

b. _____ .

3.20 Which can of stew has the most potatoes? _____

3.21 According to percentage weight, does the Beef and Vegetable can contain more water or more beef? _____

38

We have seen that pictures or words on the front of the label can show what to expect inside the can. Many labels have pictures on them that show how the food can be served. For example, most cereal boxes show a big bowl of cereal covered in delicious-looking fruit. Some pictures even go further and picture the whole breakfast with juice, toast, and a glass of milk beside the cereal bowl. What a great way to sell a product!

Labels should have preparation directions on them and many have recipes and suggestions for serving. Labels should include information on how to store the product and the total weight of the contents.

Nutritional labeling is required for products labeled "Fortified" or "Enriched." "Fortified" means that the quantity of one or more nutrients, naturally present in a lesser amount, has been increased. "Enriched" describes the addition of one or more nutrients which are not naturally present. Look at a carton of milk, for example. It often says that it is "fortified" with Vitamins A and D.

Labels should give the nutrients found in the product, the number of calories, number of calories from fat per serving, and the serving size. They provide the percentage of the daily requirement of nutrients. Nutritional labeling, then, provides a basis of comparison of the nutritive values of the food you buy.

Check for information concerning special diet requirements as well. It is important to check the ingredients on the label for anything that might cause a family member to have an allergic reaction.

Label reading can be a challenge, especially when unfamiliar ingredients must be identified. Standard ingredients must be listed by their common names (salt, for example, instead of sodium chloride), but there are no common names for some ingredients which are added to keep foods fresh or to stabilize the texture, enhance flavor and color.

Labels are an important part of every product you purchase. Read them carefully.

Answer the following questions.

3.22 List two things a label should include besides the ingredients. a. _____ and

b. _____ .

3.23 Define:

a. Fortified _____

_____

b. Enriched _____

_____

3.24 _____ ingredients must be listed by their common names.

FOOD STORAGE

Food is one of the largest items in the family budget, so it is well worth shopping around for good quality foods at a reasonable price. Because you have spent both time and money to purchase food items, it only makes sense to learn to store them properly; to keep them from spoilage.

Refrigeration can substantially reduce the rate at which food will deteriorate. Low temperatures slow down the growth of microorganisms and the rate of chemical changes in food. The diagram gives a guide to temperature likely to be found in different parts of a refrigerator set at the middle temperature range. The following storage guide can help you use your refrigerator to the best advantage.

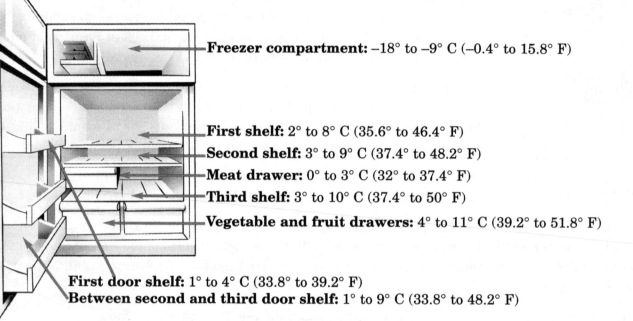

Freezer compartment: –18° to –9° C (–0.4° to 15.8° F)

First shelf: 2° to 8° C (35.6° to 46.4° F)
Second shelf: 3° to 9° C (37.4° to 48.2° F)
Meat drawer: 0° to 3° C (32° to 37.4° F)
Third shelf: 3° to 10° C (37.4° to 50° F)
Vegetable and fruit drawers: 4° to 11° C (39.2° to 51.8° F)

First door shelf: 1° to 4° C (33.8° to 39.2° F)
Between second and third door shelf: 1° to 9° C (33.8° to 48.2° F)

MEAT

Uncooked minced meat, liver, kidneys, poultry, and seafood need careful storage. Always store these foods in the coldest part of the refrigerator as close as possible to 0° C (32°F). The longest recommended storage time is three days.

Wrapped fresh meat can be kept safely for up to three days and unwrapped fresh meat up to five days at cold temperatures 0° to 3°C (32° to 38°F).

Whole red meats (for example, a leg of lamb) and cured meats have a longer storage life, and unwrapped meats last longer than wrapped meats.

Wrapped meat maintains its original high water content and quality but will spoil and an "off" odor can become apparent. The safe thing to do is to throw it out.

Cured meats can last up to three weeks.

Unwrapped meat keeps longer. Fresh meat keeps for up to five days and cured meat keeps for up to three weeks at 0° to 3°C (32° to 38°F). After time, unwrapped meat dries out, the color changes and there is a loss of flavor, yet this is preferable to meat going bad because it is wrapped.

Giblets should be removed from poultry, wrapped loosely and stored separately. Remove stuffing and meat from bones of cooked poultry as soon as possible; chill and cover or wrap separately. Fish should be stored in plastic zipper bags or a tightly covered container in the refrigerator. Refer to the recommended refrigeration storage chart on the next page.

Recommended refrigeration storage temperatures for some foods		
FOOD	**STORAGE TEMP. °C**	**SHELF LIFE IN THE HOME**
Seafood	0 – 3	3 days
Crustaceans and mollusks	0 – 3	2 days
Meat	0 – 3	3–5 days
Minced meat	0 – 3	2–3 days
Cured meat	0 – 3	2–3 weeks
Poultry	0 – 3	3 days
Fruit juices	0 – 7	7–14 days
Milk	1 – 7	5–7 days
Cream	1 – 7	5 days
Cheese	0 – 7	Variable (1–3 months)
Butter	0 – 7	8 weeks
Oil and fat	2 – 7	Variable (6 months)
Margarine	2 – 7	Variable (6 months)

FRESH FRUIT

Fresh fruits should be sorted to remove any injured fruit before storing. Refrigerate ripe tomatoes, apples, oranges, lemons, grapefruit, limes, kumquats, tangerines, peaches, apricots, cherries, grapes, pears, plums, and rhubarb in a loosely covered container or perforated plastic zipper bag to reduce wilting and drying. Store bananas, melons, avocados, and pineapple at cool room temperature. Store berries in the refrigerator dry; wash before serving.

To ripen fruit, place in a well-ventilated area at room temperature; avoid direct sunlight. Tomatoes, peaches, bananas, avocados, pears, and plums can be ripened. Refrigerate ripened fruit, except bananas, until you are ready to use them.

FRESH VEGETABLES

Potatoes, sweet potatoes, onions, and winter squash should be stored unwashed in a cool, dry dark place with good ventilation. Wash and thoroughly drain salad greens, celery, green onions, asparagus, and cabbage; refrigerate in individual zip-lock bags. Husked sweet corn may be refrigerated in zip-lock bags for a short period of time. Leave peas in the pod and refrigerate.

DAIRY PRODUCTS, EGGS

Cottage cheese, hard cheese, milk, and butter should be tightly covered and stored in the refrigerator. Store strong-flavored cheeses, such as Limburger, refrigerated in a tightly covered jar. Eggs are stored in a covered container or the original carton in the refrigerator. Egg yolks can be refrigerated in a tightly covered container for two to three days. Egg whites keep for a week to ten days refrigerated in a tightly covered container.

DEHYDRATED OR DRIED FOODS, NUTS

Dehydrated foods do not readily go bad while dry, but they are deteriorating slowly all the time, particularly once the packets are open to the air. Dehydration inhibits the growth of microbes by removing water, but it does not make foods

41

sterile and these foods may carry a high level of contaminating microorganisms which become active again in the presence of water. Rehydrated dried foods—those to which water has been added—need to be treated as highly perishable and kept in the refrigerator.

Store dried foods in a tightly closed container in a cool place away from obvious sources of heat such as a stove or direct sunlight.

Nuts will keep longer if refrigerated in tightly covered containers. Unshelled and unsalted nuts stay fresher.

CANNED FOODS

Most canned foods have been sterilized during processing and the cans need only to be stored in a cool, dry place. Watch for swollen, dented or damaged cans. This indicates a problem and possible contamination.

FLOUR, CEREALS, AND PASTA

Store at room temperature in tight containers.

Freezing food and holding it at a very low temperature, around −18°C (0°F) almost completely stops deterioration. Thawing, or even a rise in temperature without thawing, stimulates chemical and microbiological activity and spoilage may occur. Remember, frozen foods should be put in the freezer as soon as you get home from the store. Frozen foods should be thawed in the refrigerator. Generally speaking, thawed food should not be refrozen. It can be stored safely in the refrigerator for up to 48 hours if it has been thawed properly under controlled conditions in the refrigerator.

Answer the following questions.

3.25   What effect does low temperatures have on microorganisms? _____

3.26   What is the coolest section of the refrigerator (not freezer)? _____

3.27   What is the warmest section of the refrigerator? _____

3.28   Define:

a. cured_____

_____

b. deterioration_____

_____

3.29   Which keeps longer in the refrigerator, wrapped meat or unwrapped meat?_____

3.30   Do potatoes have to be refrigerated? _____

3.31   How do you store peas? _____

3.32 How long can margarine be stored in the refrigerator? _____

3.33 How long can meat be stored in the refrigerator? _____

3.34 Why are dehydrated foods less likely to spoil? _____

_____

3.35 At what temperature should your freezer be kept? _____

3.36 What is the safest way to thaw frozen foods? _____

Check which fruits can be ripened.

3.37   a. _____ tomato

     b. _____ pineapple

     c. _____ cherries

     d. _____ peaches

     e. _____ avocados

     f. _____ berries

     g. _____ melons

     h. _____ plums

Before you take the last Self Test, you may want to do one or more of these self checks.

1. _____ Read the objectives. Determine if you can do them.

2. _____ Restudy the material related to any objectives that you cannot do.

3. _____ Use the SQ3R study procedure to review the material.
   a. **S**can the sections.
   b. **Q**uestion yourself again.
   c. **R**ead to answer your questions.
   d. **R**ecite the answers to yourself.
   e. **R**eview areas you didn't understand.

4. _____ Review all vocabulary, activities, and Self Tests, writing a correct answer for each wrong answer.

SELF TEST 3

Answer the following questions (each answer, 5 points).

3.01 What is the first step in smart food shopping? _____

_____

3.02 How can you cut costs but not nutrients when food shopping? _____

_____

3.03 If a store runs out of a sale item, you may ask for a _____ .

3.04   What tells you that a dairy product is not an imitation?_____

_____

3.05   When is the best time to buy fresh fruit and vegetables? _____

_____

3.06   What is the rule for determining the amount of the ingredients as written on the label?

_____

_____

Choose the correct answer for each statement (each answer, 3 points).

3.07   Which of the following items should not be found on a label? _____
        a.   serving size and number
        b.   nutritional information
        c.   chemical names for standard ingredients
        d.   preparation instructions

3.08   Which of the following words signifies that a label lists additional nutrients which are not natu-
        rally present? _____
        a.   enriched
        b.   fortified
        c.   pasteurized
        d.   none of the above

3.09   Which kitchen layout is the least efficient? _____
        a.   L-shaped
        b.   U-shaped
        c.   Corridor
        d.   One wall

3.010   You can store foods in the freezer for _____ .
        a.   1–2 years
        b.   3–6 months
        c.   6 months–1 year
        d.   2–3 years

3.011   The small kitchen appliance that is used to puree soups, sauces, and other liquids is the _____ .
        a.   hand mixer
        b.   stand mixer
        c.   electric grinder
        d.   blender

3.012 The primary ingredient in a cookie recipe is _____ .
  a. flour
  b. sugar
  c. eggs
  d. liquid

3.013 How many teaspoons are there in 1/4 cup? _____
  a. 16
  b. 9
  c. 12
  d. 4

3.014 _____ means to plunge food into boiling water for a brief time to remove skin.
  a. Broil
  b. Blanch
  c. Julienne
  d. Poach

3.015 How long can margarine be stored? _____
  a. 3 months
  b. 6 months
  c. 9 months
  d. 1 year

Answer *true* or *false* (each answer, 3 points).

3.016 _____ A bargain is not always a bargain when food shopping.

3.017 _____ Preparing food yourself instead of buying prepared food is usually cheaper.

3.018 _____ Fresh ingredients are typically more flavorful than canned products.

3.019 _____ Sirloin cuts of meat have more protein than chuck.

3.020 _____ Cuts of meat containing less fat are more tender.

3.021 _____ Low temperatures slow down the growth of microorganisms.

3.022 _____ The coolest part of the refrigerator is the vegetable drawer.

3.023 _____ Wrapped meat keeps longer than unwrapped meat.

3.024 _____ Bananas should be kept in the refrigerator.

3.025 _____ Potatoes do not have to be refrigerated.

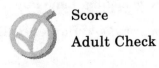

70 / 87

Score _____

Adult Check _____

Initial   Date

45

GLOSSARY

aesthetic. Pertaining to the sense of the beautiful.

convection. Transfer of heat by the circulation of movement of the heated parts of a liquid or gas.

cured. A method or process of preserving meat or fish, etc., as smoking or salting.

dehydrated. When water has been removed from vegetables, fruits, etc., for preservation.

deteriorate. To make or become worse; make or become lower in character, quality, value, etc.

fermentation. A change brought about by fermenting, like yeast enzymes, that converts grape sugar into ethyl alcohol or, in the case in bread-making, the release of carbon dioxide.

gluten. The sticky substance that holds the dough mixture together.

immersible. The ability of an item to be placed under water.

inflation. A substantial rise of prices caused by an undue expansion in paper money or bank credit.

lard. Pork fat.

leavening. An agent used to produce fermentation in dough or batter.

microbes. Microorganism, especially pathogenic bacteria.

microbiological. Anything pertaining to the structure, function, and uses of microscopic organisms.

microorganisms. Microscopic plants or animals.

radiant heat. Heat energy transmitted by electromagnetic waves in contrast to heat transmitted by conduction or convection.

rehydrate. When water is put back into any substance, for example dried foods.

tang. In a knife, the part of the blade extending into the handle.

tenderize. To make soft or delicate by pounding or by means of a chemical process or treatment.

yeast. A leavening agent used in bread dough.

BIBLIOGRAPHY

Betty Crocker's New Cookbook, Macmillan, NY, eighth edition, 1998.

The Better Business Bureau, *Guide to Wise Buying,* The Benjamin Company Inc., NY, 1980.

Rosso, Julee and Lukin, Sheila, *The New Basics Cookbook,* Workman Publishing, NY, 1989.

Samtur, Susan J., *Cashing In at the Checkout*, The Stonesong Press, NY, 1979.

Sunset Kitchens, *Planning and Remodeling*, Lane Pub. Co., CA, 1983.

Wessinger, Joanna, *The Home Answer Book,* Harper Collins Publishers, NY, 1995.

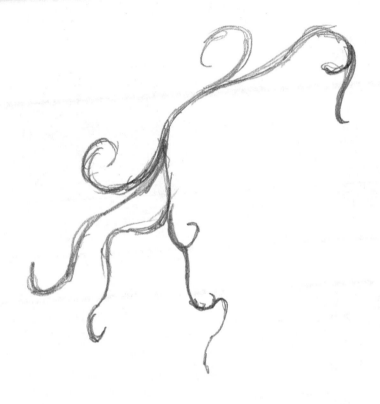

FAMILY AND CONSUMER SCIENCE LIFEPAC 7
YOUR HOME AND YOU

CONTENTS

Author: **Marcia Parker, M.Ed.**
Editor: Alan Christopherson, M.S.
Illustrations: Alpha Omega Graphics

Alpha Omega Publications®

804 N. 2nd Ave. E., Rock Rapids, IA 51246-1759
© MM by Alpha Omega Publications, Inc.   All rights reserved.
LIFEPAC is a registered trademark of Alpha Omega Publications, Inc.

CONTENTS

YOUR HOME AND YOU

Learning to entertain and demonstrate proper etiquette while keeping your first priority, which is the comfort of your guest(s), will be a major part of this LIFEPAC®. Whether you are entertaining guests for a short engagement such as a party, tea, or dinner; or you are having an overnight guest, the rule remains the same: their comfort and needs must come first.

Travel is a major part of our society today. Being a polite traveler requires effort and consideration. Learning a few rules of travel etiquette will be an important lesson for you. One other area that will interest most teens will also be discussed—dating etiquette.

With every privilege and gift comes responsibility. Taking care of what God has so richly blessed us with is an obligation and honor. The last section of this LIFEPAC will address this by teaching about home and auto maintenance and repair.

OBJECTIVES

Read these objectives. The objectives tell you what you will be able to do when you have successfully finished this LIFEPAC.

When you have finished this LIFEPAC, you should be able to:

1. Gain an understanding of how to plan for entertaining.
2. Describe different types of entertainment.
3. Demonstrate skill in planning your own social event.
4. Gain an understanding of how to prepare for and entertain overnight guests.
5. Gain knowledge concerning social graces such as table etiquette and conversation.
6. Learn about proper travel etiquette.
7. Gain knowledge concerning proper dating etiquette.
8. Learn techniques used in home maintenance and repairs.
9. Demonstrate skill in housecleaning.
10. Learn techniques used in auto maintenance and repairs.
11. Demonstrate skill in selected auto care projects.

Survey the LIFEPAC. Ask yourself some questions about the study. Write your questions here.

_____

_____

_____

_____

_____

_____

_____

Note: All vocabulary words in this LIFEPAC appear in **boldface** print the first time they are used. If you are unsure of the meaning when you are reading, study the definitions given in the glossary.

I. HOSPITALITY

The dictionary defines *hospitality* as *the receiving and treating of guests and strangers in a warm, friendly, generous way.* (Random House) Hospitality is more than proper etiquette and good conversational skills, although these are important. It involves welcoming a person into the intimate circle of your home, expressing the "spirit" of your home.

The home is the center of family life.

A house is a shelter or a place to eat and sleep, whereas a home is the center of family life. The interior design of our house exemplifies the individuality (Principle of Individuality) and our personality as the owners. However, you do not have to have religious artifacts or a picture of *Christ in the Garden of Gethsemane* hanging on your wall to show others you are a Christian. It is the home atmosphere demonstrated by the people of the home, showing generosity of spirit and genuine concern for the welfare of others, that will be the mirror reflecting the image of Christ to the visitor or guest. This is an example of the principles of Christian character in action.

Section Objectives

Review these objectives. When you have completed this section, you should be able to:

1. Gain an understanding of how to plan for entertaining.
2. Describe different types of entertainment.
3. Demonstrate skill in planning your own social event.
4. Gain an understanding of how to prepare for and entertain overnight guests.

PLANNING TO ENTERTAIN

Everyone likes to get together with friends, whether they are spending time with their best friends or getting to know new friends better. Entertaining friends almost always requires serving some sort of food, even if it is only chips, dip, and soda. Entertaining can be done almost anywhere—in a big beautiful dining room, a small apartment, a restaurant, or a club—and it can be done on a limited budget. Warmth, enthusiasm, and overall spirit is what makes it a success.

"Sorry about the dessert, folks!"

Entertaining can be fun and takes only a little work and creativity. It does require a good deal of planning, however. The advantages of detailed planning are numerous: confidence gained, money, time, energy saved, and calamities avoided (although there may be some unexpected issues). The success of any party depends largely on the style and personality of the host/hostess.

Steps in planning

Step One: Decide on the guest list.

Decide on how many guests to invite. The final decision depends on the capacity of your home (seating, table appointments, etc.) and how many people do you think you can handle. Your guest list also depends on the purpose for giving the party. For an evening of good conversation, you should limit your guest number to ten or less. For a game party or a party to introduce newcomers to friends, ten to twelve is a comfortable number. For an open house, reception, or drop-in, you can invite more than your home can hold and stagger the invitation hours.

Choosing whom to invite can be as challenging as deciding on how many guests to invite. Find common bonds such as activities, interests, and occupations. Invite some guests that like to talk and some that like to listen. Invite at least a few people who already know each other to reduce the burden on the host and hostess. Don't be afraid to mix age groups unless the situation or activity would prohibit it. If you are giving a party in someone's honor, plan the guest list with that person if possible.

Going hand-in-hand with whom you invite, is the decision as to what type of party you wish to have. The number of guests will help determine this: dinner party versus a buffet party versus light snacks and appetizers. When deciding the type of party you want to have, you need to consider the ages, interests, and maybe some of your guests' favorite things. What will they be comfortable with and enjoy? Certain parties are appropriate at certain times of the day, so this must also be considered. For example, it would not be appropriate to have a tea at night. The place of the party, whether at home, outdoors, indoors, park, church social hall, or a barn, may very well dictate the type of party you have. Other important considerations when planning the type of party you want to have include your experience, capabilities, and your resources. Also consider space, entertaining equipment, budget, and the amount of help you know you can count on.

Once you have decided on what type of party to have, decide if you would like the party to have a theme. Themes provide continuity or unity to the event. Special events have built-in themes: birthday, bridal shower, baby shower, Christmas, Valentine's Day, etc. Themes should add an unusual or special touch, but they should not be forced. You can unify the event by the use of a central theme that is carried out in invitations, colors scheme, decorations, menu, activity, music, etc.

Student: as you continue through the steps for planning a party see the examples given for carrying out the Mexican theme for a "Fiesta Party."

Step Two: Decide on an invitation.

All invitations should state the following:
- ✔ date and day
- ✔ time
- ✔ type of party
- ✔ host/hostess' name
- ✔ address of the party
- ✔ phone number if you want an RSVP
- ✔ type of dress if needed for a certain activity
- ✔ RSVP or Regards Only if desired

The type of party determines the type of invitation you send. An informal or semiformal invitation should be sent ten days before the event. You may telephone to invite guests, but be sure to give all information and be careful not to put guests on the spot. Give them a day or so to answer. You may write an invitation for an informal party on personal writing paper or notes. Preprinted invitations purchased at party or card shops are appropriate and are usually designed for a specific type of occasion. One way to make your invitations special and express your creativity is to design and make your own.

Formal invitations are always handwritten, engraved, or **thermographed** on white or cream paper. They should be written in third person. Formal invitations should be sent at least two weeks ahead of time. Invitations should never be typed unless it is a very casual party or there is no other choice.

Step Three: Decide on the menu.

What food you serve is based on the type of party you are giving, whom you have invited, and the number of guests you have invited. First, the type of party will influence your menu choice based on time of day, degree of formality, and any special theme to be carried out.

When considering whom you have invited, consider what will appeal to these people. What are their favorite foods and are there any special dietary needs to consider? When considering the number of guests to be served, think about what you can manage. When serving a large crowd, be sure to prepare foods that will keep their temperature, flavor, and appeal throughout the evening. Choose foods that can be prepared efficiently, yet appealingly, in large quantities.

Select foods that can be prepared beforehand and/or do not require extensive last-minute preparation. Use your freezer and refrigerator to your advantage. Do everything possible ahead of time. Prepare foods with which you feel confident. Don't experiment. If you want to try something unfamiliar or dazzling, try it ahead of time on your family.

Fiesta Party Menu

Appetizer:	Cheese Nachos and Tortilla Chips with Salsa
Main Course:	Taco Salad
	Cheese Enchiladas
	Bean Burritos
	Chalupas
Toppings:	shredded lettuce, ground beef, shredded cheese, sliced black olives, diced tomatoes, chopped onion, jalapeño peppers, sour cream, and guacamole
Beverages:	iced tea, carbonated soft drinks, water, coffee
Dessert:	Sopapillas with honey and assorted Mexican Sweetbreads

Follow standard meal-planning guides: have a variety of foods, colors, flavors, textures, temperatures, shapes, and preparation methods. Select the main dish first, followed by the accompanying dishes.

Step Four: Decide on decorations.

The decorations include table decorations (centerpieces, place cards, etc.) and anything else you wish to use to decorate your home (doorways, mantels, small tables, etc.). The kind of decorations you use depends on the occasion and the tastes of your guests. They should help carry out the theme. They can remain simple by using a well-chosen centerpiece and well-placed accessories on doors and end tables. Decorations can also be elaborate, extensively changing the room(s) by creating an entire thematic atmosphere using sombreros, big paper flowers of bright colors, streamers, **maracas**, **piñatas**, etc. Remember, the most important part of decorating, whether simple or elaborate, is a sparkling clean house. Decorations are especially important for children.

Step Five: Decide on the activity or entertainment.

Activities can range from calm, quiet background music for dining, to conversation, or to rowdy games. Your creativity (and space if you have a small house or apartment) is the only limit to the numerous types of activities you can have at your party. Once again consider the theme, the guest, and your resources. For our theme of "Fiesta Party" it would be fun to have a group of **mariachis** or other similarly-themed group perform. Most definitely, a piñata could be the highlight of the evening for all ages.

Step Six: Schedule all preparation activities.

Assign a day to each task that needs to be done in the preparation of your party. Look for things that you can do ahead, such as grocery shopping, preparing some dishes, cleaning the house, decorating, setting the table, or polishing silver. This will save you from panicking on the day of the party.

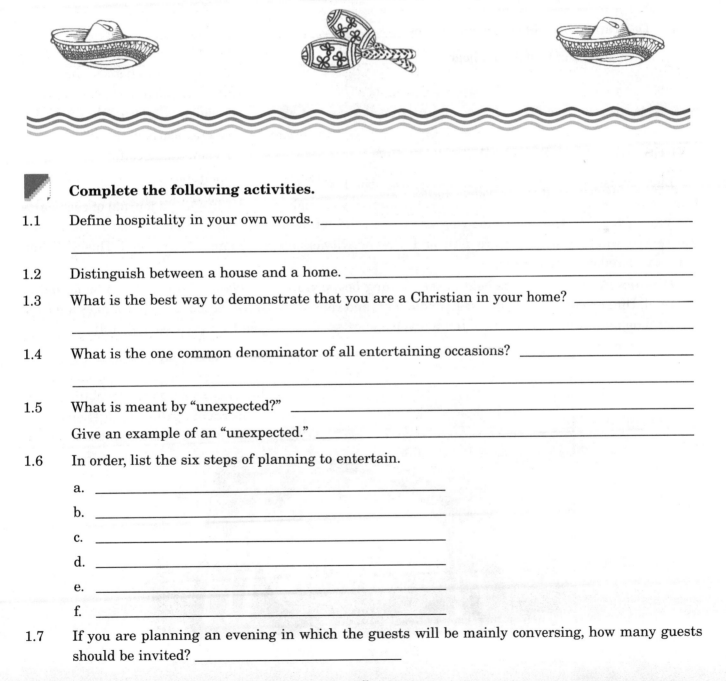

Complete the following activities.

1.1   Define hospitality in your own words. _____
_____

1.2   Distinguish between a house and a home. _____

1.3   What is the best way to demonstrate that you are a Christian in your home? _____
_____

1.4   What is the one common denominator of all entertaining occasions? _____
_____

1.5   What is meant by "unexpected?" _____

Give an example of an "unexpected." _____

1.6   In order, list the six steps of planning to entertain.

a. _____

b. _____

c. _____

d. _____

e. _____

f. _____

1.7   If you are planning an evening in which the guests will be mainly conversing, how many guests should be invited? _____

1.8   How can you accommodate more people at a reception than your house will hold? _____

_____

1.9   Is it ever a good idea to mix age groups when selecting guests to attend a party? _____

1.10   _____ provide a continuity or unity to the event.

1.11   Give an example of a built-in theme. _____

1.12   _____ invitations are always handwritten, engraved, or thermographed on white or cream paper.

1.13   The food selection of a party is based on what three things?

        a.   _____

        b.   _____

        c.   _____

1.14   Decorations should help carry out the _____ .

1.15   Give an example of a "do-ahead" task. _____

TYPES OF ENTERTAINMENT

Each occasion you plan can be different from the last. You as host/hostess and your guests will certainly enjoy the variety. If you do a lot of entertaining, you might consider keeping a journal of each party you have given. You should include who was there, who sat by whom, what theme was used, what menu was served, what decorations were used, and what activity or entertainment was provided. This will eliminate the boredom of repetition.

Dinners. A dinner party is held in the evening between five and eight o'clock and can be formal or informal. Dinner jackets, long dresses, candlelight, and refreshing conversation are what makes a formal dinner a delight. A formal dinner of ten to twelve guests will be served by a professional staff.

Butter Knife — Water Glass

Bread Plate — Beverage Glass

Dessert Fork — Dessert Spoon

Dinner Plate — Dinner Knife

Dinner Fork — Spoon

Salad Fork — Soup Spoon

Napkin

Formal Dinner Place Setting

The informal dinner is the most popular type of dinner party. Four to eight people is the easiest to manage, because there is no maid to serve your guests. With no professional help, the host and hostess will have to be well organized and willing to fill in as cook, server, and cleaner. Serving eight people without help is manageable. The trick is to plan dishes—a one-dish main course, a salad, and a dessert—that require little, if any, last-minute preparations. When you keep things more simple, you are free to spend less time worrying and more time enjoying your guests.

Brunches. The English came up with the idea of combining breakfast and lunch; thus, brunch. It is generally informal and served mid-morning—ten to twelve o'clock. It can be a sit-down or buffet style of service. It lends itself well to both family and entertaining occasions. It is especially nice for holiday entertaining. It is a good idea for bridal or baby showers and is an excellent way to entertain women with school-age children.

The menu reflects choices from breakfast and lunch. It can be simple or exotic. The meal is generally served buffet style. Food choices can include: eggs benedict, quiche, omelets, crepes, souffles, light dishes of meat, poultry or fish, waffles, pancakes, French toast, etc. Include special breads, muffins, biscuits, croissants, and brioche. Fresh fruits and pitchers of fruit juices, coffee, and hot tea should be on the buffet table as well.

Luncheons. A luncheon is typically a ladies' affair, but does not have to be. It is similar to the brunch and is a good way to entertain mothers with school-age children. It should be brief; no activity is needed.

It is best to have only two courses. The appetizer, if you have one, can be served in the living room as guests arrive. The luncheon should be light. You may use any meat, but keep the main dish light or serve only small portions. Suggested dishes are: crepes, quiche, souffles, salads, soups, casseroles. Special breads as for the brunch are a nice addition. Dessert can be richer if the meal was very light: ice cream, sherbet, frozen dessert, pastries, meringue shells, mousse, parfaits.

Suggested luncheon

Teas. The daily ritual of having afternoon tea is really a thing of the past. Men and women are usually at work during the traditional tea time, between four-thirty and five-thirty. A formal tea is most likely to be given for an official function or to honor a **debutante**. It is a very formal occasion and all guests should arrive on time. The hostess will either invite the guests to the table and will serve the tea individually to each guest; or the hostess will invite the guests to serve themselves at a buffet and sit at small tables scattered throughout the house or garden. The tea table will always have a cloth table covering and napkins. A china tea service is an absolute must for a formal tea. Dainty, exquisitely decorated finger foods (i.e. tarts, scones, butter cookies) should be served with the tea.

7

A wedding reception line

Receptions. A reception usually honors someone or celebrates an occasion such as a wedding, an engagement, a visiting dignitary, a welcome, a farewell, or congratulations. It is usually in the evening, but may be during the day. It is normally a drop-in affair at which guests converse and mingle. The guests should not stay longer than the time stated on the invitation and should speak to the guest of honor.

The food served at a reception depends on whether the reception is formal or informal. If it is formal, a buffet table is covered with a floor-length white tablecloth and platters of elaborate finger food, tea sandwiches, small cookies and pastries, along with napkins and plates. Waiters should serve beverages and plates of food around to the guests.

The food at smaller, less formal receptions might consist of cheeses, crackers, and mixed nuts. At this type of affair, drinks and punches are served from one location or may be passed around by a waiter.

When a reception is given to honor a special person(s), there should be a receiving line in which the host, hostess, guest or guests of honor stand.

Showers. Showers may be a drop-in, full-evening affair with games and devotionals, or even a shower-by-mail. It should not be given by the family and should not have too many hostesses. You may choose among four fashions of how to serve food: reception, tea, brunch, or one large dessert with a hot beverage. A shower can be given for a number of reasons.

A baby shower is usually given about a month before the baby is due. It is also appropriate to give the shower after the baby is born, so you should ask the expectant mother which she prefers. If it is known whether the baby is a boy or girl, it is good to pass this along to the guests in the invitation so that they can buy appropriate gifts. Ask the expectant mother if there are any special items that she needs, such as crib, stroller, etc. that several guests could purchase together.

Every bride-to-be enjoys being given at least one shower—perhaps not so much for the presents it brings as for the chance to get together, often for the last time as a single woman, with her closest friends. The shower is usually given by the maid-of-honor or a close friend. Gifts are usually simple and practical items ranging in price from $5.00 to $20.00, saving the more elaborate and expensive gifts for the wedding.

It is often fun to have a theme for gift giving at a bridal shower: kitchen, linen, bath, or personal. The personal shower consists of close personal friends of the same sex and includes gifts of lingerie, hosiery, and travel items. Ideas to give your shower a special touch are for guests to bring one spice along with their gift for the bride, for guests to provide one recipe along with the gift, or to write a few words of advice for the bride.

Another great idea for a wedding shower is to have a couple's shower; friends of both the bride and groom attend this type of shower. Guests bring gifts that are used by both, such as linens for bath and bed, clocks, decorative accessories, plants, tools, table games, photo albums, and appliances.

Parties. There are too many types of parties to discuss them all, but it is enough to say that people love parties and will find all sorts of occasions to celebrate: anniversary, birthday, children's, costume, engagement, farewell, graduation, office, surprise, sweet sixteen, etc.

These are only a few you can choose from, but whatever party you plan to give, remember that a party is a celebration of an accomplishment, event, or joyful occasion in someone's life. Make it a memorable, pleasant experience for all who attend.

Complete the following.

1.16 How can you eliminate the boredom of repetition in your party giving? _____

_____

1.17 What time is best for a formal dinner party? _____

1.18 How many guests is the appropriate number for a formal dinner party? _____

1.19 Why should you have fewer guests at an informal dinner than a formal dinner? _____

_____

1.20 Define brunch. _____

1.21 Plan a menu for a brunch buffet. _____

_____

_____

Answer *true* **or** *false*.

1.22 _____ A tea is a very formal occasion.

1.23 _____ The traditional tea time is between four-thirty and five-thirty.

1.24 _____ Beverages should be served by waiters at receptions.

1.25 _____ The food served at a formal reception is more elaborate than at an informal reception.

1.26 _____ A baby shower should always be given before the baby is born.

Answer the following.

1.27 Give an example of an appropriate gift for a baby shower that guests can purchase together.

_____

1.28 What is the price range for an average bridal shower gift? _____

1.29 What can you do to give a shower a special touch? _____

_____

1.30 Is it appropriate to give a wedding shower for the couple? _____

1.31 What is the general rule for a gift that is appropriate for a couple's shower? _____

_____

Give an example. _____

Complete the following activity.

1.32 Using the steps for planning to entertain, select one of the types of entertainment and plan a party on paper. You do not have to give a party or purchase anything. Decide on a theme other than Mexican Fiesta Party and write out your plans in detail, including the menu. Design and make your own invitations and decorations. At least, describe your decorations.

Adult Check _____

Initial   Date

OVERNIGHT GUESTS

Overnight guests fall into two categories: formal and informal. Family and close friends are considered informal, whereas a visiting missionary would be considered a formal guest. The role of host and hostess are much different today as compared to several years ago.

The role of the host.[1] As the host, it is your responsibility to offer your house guest a clean, comfortable, warm, and well-furnished guest room. The two priorities for the guest quarters would be privacy and cleanliness. To provide privacy for your guests, be sure that there is a lock on the door and draperies and/or shades at the windows. They should have no fears of anyone walking in on them or of being seen from outside. The ideal situation is to have a guest bedroom that is kept prepared for guests at all times. The best way to see if your guest room is comfortable and will satisfy the most meticulous guest is to give it a test run by sleeping in it yourself. The guest bedroom should have twin beds with a nightstand between them. This arrangement will meet the needs of several different situations. However, one option

---

[1] The term "host" will be used throughout this section to encompass both the host and hostess.

10

is to let your guest use the master bedroom. This should be done only if you are able to manage the household well and not disrupt guests frequently. Another option is to let your guest use a family member's room. Of course you will have to rearrange sleeping and closet accommodations. Children will have to be reminded to keep out and not bother the guest. As a last resort you may have to put the guest in a den, family room, or living room. You will still need to arrange for privacy so that neither party suffers embarrassment. Consider setting up privacy screens.

Checklist for Guest Bedroom. Make your guest feel comfortable, and have the room prepared as best you can. Clean linens, sheets, blanket, a spread or comforter, and pillows make a good start. You may need to have extra blankets if the weather is cool. If possible, have ample closet and drawer space and hangers for your guest. If this is not feasible, at least have a space where your guest may put their suitcase or garment bag without being in the way. Refer to the checklist of other touches a considerate host may use.

Formal Guest Bedroom Checklist

- ✔ Good lighting (include a bedside lamp)
- ✔ Mirror
- ✔ Clock with alarm
- ✔ Facial tissues
- ✔ Wastebasket
- ✔ Sewing kit with safety pins
- ✔ Radio/TV
- ✔ Plastic bag for dirty laundry
- ✔ Clothes brush
- ✔ Magazines, books
- ✔ Flowers/plant
- ✔ Telephone, telephone book
- ✔ Iron, ironing board (or tell the guest where these are kept)
- ✔ Desk
- ✔ Pad and pencil on bedside table
- ✔ Note paper/envelopes/stamps

Having house guests for a night, for a cozy winter weekend, or for a leisurely summer weekend is a wonderful way to catch up with friends or visit with family in the relaxed atmosphere of your home. With house guests such as family and friends, your main concern should be that they feel at home and feel free to help themselves to any and all things that they may want or need. The items listed in the checklist are only a suggestion and are not always available for individual guest use. Always make sure your guests know where to find items that were not available in their bedrooms. Some of these items include: telephone and telephone books, iron and ironing board, plastic bags for dirty laundry or washer and dryer, sewing kit, snacks, kitchen items, etc. Having house guests should not be stressful for either the guest or the host.

Checklist for Guest Bathroom. The checklist for the guest bathroom is only an indication of what should be available to your guest. Most guests will supply most of these items themselves, but just in case they have forgotten something, you could have it on hand or at least let them know where they could be purchased. The ideal situation would be for the guest to have his own bathroom attached or very close to his bedroom. If this is not possible, assign them one to use separate from the family. Once again if this is not possible, then be sure to give guests some indication of the best time to shower so they will not be waiting. When your guests arrive at your home, show them their room and bathroom. Tell them (without getting tedious) what they need to know: closet and drawer space, where and how the lights work, how to set the alarm clock, where to find extra linens and towels, how to work the shower controls, how to adjust the heating and cooling controls.

Guest Bathroom Checklist

✔ Face towel, bath towel, washcloth, bath mat
✔ Place a towel rack for the guest's towels in their bedroom if the bathroom is not separate from the rest of the family.
✔ New soaps for basin and bathtub, plus liquid soap
✔ Bath oil and bath powder
✔ Shampoo and conditioner
✔ Hand creams
✔ Facial tissue
✔ Paper cups
✔ A few medicines, aspirin, adhesive bandage strips, sun block, antacid, etc.
✔ Toothbrushes and toothpaste
✔ Mouthwash
✔ Razors
✔ Blow dryer
✔ Heating pad
✔ Extra toilet tissue
✔ Feminine hygiene products
✔ Wastebasket
✔ Air freshener
✔ Night light

Respect your guests' need for privacy, time schedules, and rest, but offer fellowship. Don't expect them to sit up late talking, playing games, etc. or to spend the entire day with you. Don't make it hard for them to get away if you can tell that they are very tired. Schedule meals and other activities for them according to their needs. Be on time yourself. Keep the children and any pets from being bothersome. Ask if you can do anything for them and then mention specifics such as laundry, ironing, errands (shoe, shop, dry cleaners, drugstore, post office). Provide a shelf in the refrigerator for them to use. Be alert and sensitive to any special needs that your guest may have such as illnesses or special diet. Don't insist they eat and eat and eat.

If your guests are planning an extended stay, offer activities. Give them a tourist list and advice. Don't plan too much. Let them choose whether or not they want to go on their own or have you take them. Provide them with a city map and directions to sightseeing places, the post office, stores, malls, etc. Provide them with a house key and offer transportation. Don't forget to change the bed linens and towels as needed.

The role of the guest. When a friend invites you to be a house guest overnight or for a weekend, respond promptly. Be on time, above everything else. Do not arrive more than five to ten minutes early. Call ahead if something unavoidable will hinder your getting there on time. If you are going to be considerably late, make sure it is for a very good reason.

Be pleasant and agreeable in all circumstances. Be mature. Participate, contribute, and give. Converse with others. Be friendly—meet new people if there are other guests. Participate in games and activities. Be a good sport if you lose. Do not expect to be entertained constantly. Also, do not monopolize every conversation. It is give and take. Don't brag. Be genuine, but be your best self.

Observe all appropriate rules of courtesy, etiquette, and **decorum**. Eat what is set before you, even if you don't care for it. Explain privately to the hostess if you cannot eat something for medical reasons, but make it clear you expect no special attention. Observe all rules at the table and in interaction with others.

Help if appropriate. Don't offer if you notice hired help. Offer if there is no help, but do not insist if the host declines. She may not want to have to watch you and the dinner. Offer last-minute help with pouring beverages, lighting candles, etc. Many hosts will accept this kind of help when they won't accept other kinds. Offer to help clean up after dinner. However, the host may not wish to clean up immediately; so do not force her to by insisting on helping.

Let your hostess know you appreciate all she has done: her kindness in inviting you, her work in preparing the meal, her gracious hospitality. Thank her in person, but do not overdo it or embarrass her. Write a note after you get home or at least mention how much you appreciated the hospitality the next time you talk with her. Thank you notes are obligatory for overnight stays, a meal, or an occasion at which you were the guest of honor. Thank-you notes are optional for an open house or shower.

July 10, 20__
Dear Sue,
Thank you for your gracious hospitality. I had a wonderful time visiting you.
Love,
Mary

Give a gift if appropriate. You need not give a gift for social occasions. In some places, it is customary to send flowers the day of the party. You should give the gift when you arrive. You should be sure the gift suits the hostess' taste. Don't make her feel as though she must bring it out every time you visit. Refer to the table for some gift ideas.

GIFT IDEAS FOR THE HOST/HOSTESS

Consumable items:
- Decorative soaps
- Candy
- Flowers
- Fruit
- Cheese package
- Something from your garden
- Assortment of gift wrappings and gift cards for various occasions

Seasonal items:
- Christmas tree ornament
- Poinsettia plant
- Easter lily

Miscellaneous items:
- Candles
- Beautiful paper napkins, doilies, place cardholders, trays—anything used for entertaining
- Book
- Recording
- Padded satin hangers
- Scented drawer liners
- Games

Learning to exit gracefully takes practice. Don't eat and run; however, be considerate of the host's schedule and observe the time she planned for the occasion to end. She has cleaning up to do and needs rest. Observe these general guides for length of stay. Never stay past midnight.

Drop-in visit:	30 minutes
Lunch:	1/2 hour after meal
Dinner:	2 hours after meal

MANNERS FOR HOUSEGUEST
Don't come unannounced and uninvited.
Don't overstay. It is better to end a visit while everyone is still enjoying it!
Arrive on time and be on time for the activities and meals scheduled during your visit.
Let the host know exactly who will be coming. Don't bring your pets.
Be adaptable, agreeable, pleasant, and mature in all circumstances.
Keep your room and bathroom immaculate. Don't use more than your share of hot water or bathroom time.
Don't criticize the community, state, church, or friends of those with whom you are staying.
Respect the privacy of the home. Don't look into closets, drawers, etc.
Don't expect to sit back and be entertained while in someone's home as an overnight guest or a guest for a meal. Take an active part in conversation. Ask questions. Get to know your host.
Leave everything (when you leave the home) in the room and bathroom as you found it.
Leave a written note of thanks or send one back to the host as soon as you get home or as soon as possible when traveling.

Complete the following.

1.33 List two priorities of the guest quarters. a. _____ and b. _____

1.34 The ideal bed and bath situation for guest accommodations would be _____ _____ .

1.35 How can you as the host make sure that the guest bedroom is comfortable and will satisfy your guest? _____

1.36 What kind of bed is ideal for a guest bedroom? _____

1.37 List five essentials for a guest bedroom.

a. _____

b. _____

c. _____

d. _____

e. _____

14

1.38 List five essentials for a guest bathroom.

a. _____

b. _____

c. _____

d. _____

e. _____

1.39 What is the first thing you do when your guest arrives at your house? _____

_____

Answer *true* **or** *false*.

1.40 _____ You should plan extensive activities for your guests so there is not a moment of boredom.

1.41 _____ You should expect to be with your guests at all times.

1.42 _____ As a guest, you should always insist upon helping the host.

Complete these activities.

1.43 As a houseguest, you should observe all appropriate rules of _____ , etiquette and

_____ .

1.44 When is a thank-you note necessary? _____

_____

1.45 When do you give a thank-you gift to the host? _____

1.46 Nancy was invited to dinner at Sally's house. How long is it appropriate for her to stay?

_____

1.47 Is it okay to investigate your host's house so that you can get to know them better? _____

Complete the following activity.

1.48 You were invited to a weekend house party at a friend's house. Write a thank you note to the host.

_____
_____
_____
_____
_____

Adult Check _____

                    Initial   **Date**

Review the material in this section in preparation for the Self Test. The Self Test will check your mastery of this particular section. The items missed on this Self Test will indicate specific areas where restudy is needed for mastery.

15

SELF TEST 1

Match the terms (each answer, 3 points).

1.01 _____ a shelter or a place to eat   a. brunch

1.02 _____ provides continuity to an event   b. do ahead

1.03 _____ common denominator for any party   c. food

1.04 _____ cleaning the house   d. home

1.05 _____ 10-12 o'clock; midmorning   e. house

1.06 _____ 4:30-5:30; late afternoon   f. tea

1.07 _____ uninvited guest   g. theme

1.08 _____ center of family life   h. unexpected

Choose the correct letter (each answer, 3 points).

1.09 _____ is a comfortable number of guests for an evening of good conversation.
   a. Ten or less   b. Ten to twelve
   c. Thirteen to fifteen

1.010 When deciding whom to invite to a party, you should consider which of the following? _____
   a. ages, interests, and favorites of guests   b. time of the party
   c. the place the party is to be held   d. all of the above

1.011 You can accommodate more people at an open house than your house will hold by _____ .
   a. hoping everyone won't come that said they would
   b. staggering the invitation hours
   c. requesting some of your close friends take the lead and leave early

1.012 Which of the following is not a built-in theme? _____
   a. birthday   b. anniversary
   c. barbecue   d. bridal shower

1.013 Which of the following is true about a shower? _____
   a. It is usually given by a family member.
   b. Gifts are usually simple and practical for a bridal shower.
   c. A baby shower is usually given one week before the baby is due.

1.014 You do not have a separate guest bedroom. Which of the following order of choices is correctly listed from best to worst? _____
   a. master bedroom, family member's bedroom, family room
   b. family member's bedroom, master bedroom, family room
   c. family room, master bedroom, family member's room

1.015 A thank you note must be sent for _____ .
   a. shower   b. open house
   c. overnight stay   d. all of the above

1.016 Bill dropped in to see Sarah. How long is it appropriate for him to stay? _____
   a. 15 minutes   b. 30 minutes
   c. one hour

16

Answer *true* **or** *false* (each answer, 3 points).

1.017 _____ A formal invitation should never be typed.

1.018 _____ A party is a good time to make that new recipe you have been wanting to try.

1.019 _____ It is appropriate to mix age groups when planning the guest list.

1.020 _____ A formal dinner is usually served by a professional staff.

1.021 _____ Hot tea is best when served in china tea cups.

1.022 _____ A reception is usually in the afternoon.

1.023 _____ It is inappropriate to give a couple's shower.

1.024 _____ The two priorities for the guest quarters are privacy and cleanliness.

1.025 _____ The best way to see if your guest room is comfortable is to have the guests fill out a questionnaire before they leave.

1.026 _____ You should plan daily activities for extended staying guests.

Define the following words (each answer, 5 points).

1.027 hospitality

_____

_____

1.028 decorum

_____

_____

Short Answer (12 points).

1.029   How are hospitality and Christian character related?

_____

_____

_____

_____

II. ETIQUETTE

How many times have you felt unsure of yourself? You were unsure what was expected of you; you felt your actions and words were on trial. It is possible to fake confidence, to pretend you are cool and in the "know." But faking it can be stressful, since you are constantly afraid that you will be "found out." Hopefully, what you will learn from this section of LIFEPAC 7 will prepare you for most social situations. Etiquette provides the knowledge and gives the confidence you need to pass some tests of life.

Section Objectives

Review these objectives. When you have completed this section, you should be able to:

5. Gain knowledge concerning social graces such as table etiquette and conversation.

6. Learn about proper travel etiquette.

7. Gain knowledge concerning proper dating etiquette.

TABLE ETIQUETTE AND CONVERSATION

There is no escaping the need for good table manners. Knowing how to act at a dinner table will make it easier for you to be a guest or a gracious host.[1] You will make a favorable impression on others and enjoy yourself while doing so.

Is this your table etiquette?

---

[1] The term "host" will be used throughout this section to encompass both the host and hostess.

Do	Don't
Sit up straight in your chair.	Do not lean over or slouch over the table
Gentlemen, make sure all women are seated before you sit.	Don't stuff too much food in your mouth.
Keep hands in your lap when you are not eating.	Don't talk with your mouth full.
Elbows may rest gently on the edge of the table between courses only.	Don't take up more than your fair share of elbow space.
Wait for food to be passed to you.	Never reach across the table for something; ask someone to pass it.
Cut your salad rather than shoving a big lettuce leaf into your mouth.	Never chew with your mouth open or make loud noises when you eat.
Cut only enough meat for two or three bites at a time.	Don't lower your mouth to the food; lift your food to your mouth.
Spoon soup away from you when you spoon it out of the bowl.	Do not slurp your soup.
Place used tea bags beside your cup on your saucer.	Do not slurp your coffee or tea.
Use your knife or a piece of bread to push food onto your fork.	Do not use your fingers to push food onto your fork.
Fold your napkin loosely and leave it beside your plate when you are finished eating.	Don't leave lipstick marks on cup or glass; use lipstick moderately when dining.
Let host know ahead of time if you have special eating requirements (diets).	
Ask your host for another piece of flatware if you drop yours onto the floor. It is usually too difficult to retrieve it from under the table during a meal.	

The Do's and Don'ts of Table Etiquette

Napkin smarts. The meal begins when the host starts to unfold her napkin. This the signal for you to do the same. When she takes her first bite, you may begin eating. Place the napkin in your lap. A napkin is not a bib, unless you are under the age of two. Never use your napkin as a handkerchief unless it is an absolute emergency, especially if it is made of cloth. The host will signal the end of the meal by placing her napkin on the table.

From time to time while dining, you will encounter some embarrassing situations. Here are some pointers to help you out.

Spills. If you spill on your clothes, quietly wipe it off with your napkin; you may use a little water from your water glass. Don't draw attention to yourself by crying, shouting, or getting upset. If you spill on the tablecloth, tell your hostess so she can take the proper steps to prevent staining. Don't cover it up with your plate.

Removing unwanted food. If the food is hot enough to burn your mouth or tongue, taking a drink of water or other cold beverage is the best way to remain calm, cool, and collected. If you find a bone, fruit pit, or gristle while chewing, remove it the same way it went in: place it on your fork and then onto the side of your plate. Fish bones can be removed easier with the thumb and forefinger. Don't spit food into your napkin, especially if it is made of cloth.

Sneezing at the table. Your nose starts to tingle and itch, your eyes water—you are about to sneeze. There is nothing you can do to stop it, but you can prevent offending others. Turn your head away from the table and away from all others if possible, and put your handkerchief or hand over your mouth and nose when you sneeze. Do not blow your nose at the table; excuse yourself and leave the room.

Toothpicks. If you have food stuck in your teeth, do not pick at it at the table; excuse yourself and go take care of it away from the table. Hand signals or facial contortions are not how you tell someone they have food stuck in their teeth. Quietly tell them. Using a toothpick is an inappropriate means of removing food in public. It is appropriate to use a toothpick in a very casual setting or with family at home.

Coping with tableware. Although this subject has been discussed before, it is important to review a few things. Remember to work from the outside to the inside when using utensils. Start with the fork, knife, or spoon that is farthest from the plate and work your way in with each successive course. Your dessert spoon and fork are located above your dinner plate.

When the knife is not in use, it should rest across the top rim of your plate with the cutting edge directed downward. When the fork or spoon is not in use, it should rest across the center of your plate, in the soup or salad bowl, or on the saucer, as the case may be. When you are finished with the flatware, never place it back on the table, tablecloth, or place mat.

Correct   **Incorrect**

Hold stemmed glasses securely at the base of the bowl of the glass, between your thumb and first two fingers. Hold a cup with one hand by the handle, not "cradled" in two hands.

The knife that is lying on the butter dish is used to remove butter from the butter plate. The pat of butter is then put on your bread and butter plate. Do not use the serving knife to spread butter on your piece of bread. Use your own knife.

It is the job of the host to get the conversation rolling, regulate it, keep it rolling, and change topics if necessary. Starting and maintaining a conversation involves not only knowing what to say and when to say it, but also knowing what not to say and when to keep quiet.

A good conversationalist is knowledgeable about a variety of topics, has a sense of humor that enables him to entertain others, laugh at himself, and be a good listener.

The conversations at dinner parties, in homes, and at restaurants can vary widely, depending upon the nature of the guests and the reason for the dinner. Start with common interests. Small talk can be a lifesaver in many situations. It fills the voids in conversations, helps ease tense moments, sets others at ease, and helps us become acquainted with others.

Do not ask questions that are too personal or intimate, such as inquiries about religious beliefs, finances, or terminal illness. Neither should you ask about someone's weight, height, shoe size, or about their age and mental health.

Spreading gossip is definitely off limits. Offensive racial and ethnic jokes are also taboo. You do not have to respond to rude or tactless questions or comments.

Complete the following.

2.1   Gentlemen should make sure that all _____ are seated before they sit down at the table.

2.2   When is it permissible to have your elbows on the table? _____

2.3   Should you cut all of your meat up at one time? _____ If no, then how much do you cut at a time? _____

2.4   What should you use to push food onto your fork? _____

2.5   What is the signal for the meal to begin? _____

_____

2.6   With what do you cover a spill on the table cloth? _____

2.7   How do you remove unwanted food from your mouth? _____

_____

2.8   Is it ever okay to use a toothpick? _____ If yes, when? _____

_____

2.9   What is the general rule for using utensils? _____

_____

2.10   Where does a used knife belong? _____

21

TRAVEL ETIQUETTE

Air travel. The two complaints most often made about air travelers are those who carry on too much luggage and crowd everyone around them and those who talk too much. Your carry-on luggage should fit easily into the overhead bin or under your seat. Call the airline you will be using if you are unsure of the sizes you need to use.

Wrong technique

Right technique

There are a number of ways to limit the amount of conversation with your seat mate. Politely apologize to them that you have work to get done or that you are in need of some shut-eye and really cannot talk. Or, you can keep your head down and concentrate on your work or simply give vague, short answers to his inquiries and hope that he will get the point. If all else fails, offer him a book or newspaper to read.

There are other little tips you should acquaint yourself with if you are going to be a polite and proper air traveler. Remember to look behind your seat before reclining so you don't hit someone's knees or head if they are bending over for some reason. Usually passengers put their seat in the upright position for mealtime. Gently lower and raise the service tray. Remember it is attached to the passenger's seat in front of you.

Thoughtless actions

Mealtime is a good time to be sociable so put your work away and try to be pleasant for a short time while you eat.

The job of the flight attendants is to ensure safety and comfort, not to be your personal maid, so don't treat them as such. Be sure to thank them as you leave the plane.

Hotel/motel stays. The most important thing to remember when staying at a motel or hotel is consideration for other guests. The walls are thin and the halls echo, so keep the noise down. Lower your voices in the hallways and don't let your room door slam shut. If your area of the hotel is a non-smoking area, please abide by this rule. If others are presenting a problem for your comfort, notify the office and let the manager handle it. If the manager is unwilling or unable to assist, dial 911.

It is very important to locate exits in case of fire or some other need for fast evacuation. The stairwells are the most important exits when you are on the second or higher floor.

Women traveling alone. Women traveling alone should always take extra precautions. Avoid dark or deserted places. Use bellhops at the hotel so they are the first to check that your room is safe and valet parking to avoid dark parking garages. Ask the desk clerk to write down your room number instead of saying it out loud. Check the door locks in the room and fire exits, and always keep your door locked from the inside. Request a room nearer to the elevator where there will be less seclusion. Today, it is a good idea to have a cellular phone with you when you are traveling alone. Above all else, be alert to what is going on around you at all times.

Answer the following questions.

2.11   What are the two most common complaints of air travelers?

a. _____

b. _____

2.12   What is the most important thing to remember when staying in a motel? _____

_____

2.13   Why should you know where and how to reach the stairwells in a hotel? _____

_____

2.14   What special piece of modern equipment is useful for a woman traveling alone?

_____

DATING ETIQUETTE

Twenty years ago, dating rules seemed clear. Boys initiated the date, always paid the dinner tab, pulled out the chair and helped seat their dates, and always opened and closed the car door after seeing their dates safely in or out of the automobile. These rules may appear old-fashioned, but both the young men and young women knew what to expect of each other.

Today things are different. Some young ladies initiate the dating. With these etiquette changes comes the need to effectively communicate one's wishes. Two books dealing with dating from a Christian perspective are, *Of Knights and Fair Maidens*, by Jeff and Danielle Myers; and *I Kissed Dating Goodbye*, by Joshua Harris.

The most important aspect of dating is still to honor your parents. Many parents are uncomfortable with the notion of one-on-one dating. If that is so, please respect your parents and wait. If your parents approve to let you date, then the following guidelines may clear up the confusion regarding the subject.

Three issues generally come up most often during dates.

Issue One: Who initiates the date?

Despite what you may think about the changes caused by the Feminist movement, the young man usually initiates the dates in America to this day. It is, however, socially acceptable for a young woman to initiate a date.

Neither young women or young men like to be **harassed** by someone with whom they have made it perfectly clear they are not interested. Respect the wishes of the individual when he/she avoids phone calls or makes excuses for not talking to or accepting a date from you. Keep in mind that just because a person is not romantically interested in you does not mean that they don't want to be friends.

One of the biggest difficulties for a young person is how to refuse an invitation for a date. Be honest about your refusal. Simply say, "I'm sorry, but I already have plans." Then when the person who asked you out sees you with another young man or young woman, they won't be surprised or hurt.

Refusing a date that you'd really like to accept requires sincere regret. Be tactful. Give a real reason for the refusal and then say "I'd really like to go out with you another time." A reason that is genuine may open the door for another date.

If an individual you aren't interested in dating persists in asking, it is better to say how you feel gently and honestly than to lead the person on indefinitely. Just say, "You know, I don't think I'm the person for you, but I'm really flattered that you asked."

Rules of etiquette when asking someone on a date.

1. Ask early. Two to four days ahead of time is sufficient for a regular date, earlier for a special occasion. Exception to this rule: A group of friends are going out for pizza and bowling and you think your friend might enjoy joining the group. Call and ask, making it clear that it is **Dutch treat**, everyone pays his own way, and there are no strings attached.

2. Always call and ask in person. Do not send a note through a mutual friend.

3. Use good timing. Don't ask for a date when the person is with a group of friends or in the middle of something important. Do not call during the dinner hour if you want to impress the parents.

4. Be specific. Never ask, "What are you doing Saturday night?" Instead say, "Would you like to go to the basketball game with me on Saturday night?" Once you have been accepted, be sure to give the time, the transportation, who else might be there (double date), what to wear, and curfew.

5. Be clear about who pays. An invitation to go out does not always mean that the person doing the inviting is paying. If you are asking and plan on paying you might say, "I'd like to treat you to miniature golf Friday night." If you can't afford to pay but want to initiate the date, you might say something such as, "I'm short on funds, but I'd love to go Dutch treat for a burger before the football game Saturday night. I can drive. Would you like to go?" If you have been invited out and you're not sure who's paying, simply say, "I'd love to go out with you. Is this Dutch treat or are you paying?" You should take enough money with you to cover any of your expenses if the need arises.

Issue Two: Who controls the date?

Some young men enjoy the "masculine" role of deciding where to go on a date. Many young women feel quite comfortable with this. In that case, there's nothing wrong with an "old-fashioned date" with the young man making the decisions. There is, however, nothing wrong with a more equal relationship where both share in decision making.

Rule of etiquette: It is important to communicate your preferences and try to come to an accommodation with your partner. Consider the other person.

Issue Three: Who pays for the date?

Despite the changes in dating etiquette, most women still expect the gentleman to pay the expenses for the date. If you're a man, expect to pay most of the time unless you both have agreed to share the expenses.

Rules of etiquette.

1. It is acceptable to go Dutch treat as long as this was discussed earlier with your date and she has agreed. It is very rude to ask a young woman to an event and then surprise her at the ticket window by making her pay for her own ticket.

2. Normally it is assumed that the young man will pay, but if you are a young woman who prefers to pay your own way, discuss this ahead of time, preferably on the phone before your first date.

3. Some young men think it unfair that they are expected to pay for all the dating expenses. Some young women feel guilty or obligated when the young man pays for everything. One way to equalize the situation is for the young man to pay for out-of-pocket expenses and the young woman to repay him by having him over for dinner or by preparing a picnic lunch for the two of them. This is a very fair way of handling the issue.

4. Again, communication and tolerance are crucial. Come to an agreement early on who is to pay.

A fancy restaurant is a nice alternative.

Fast food places are generally the restaurants teenagers are most likely familiar with and comfortable in. One waits in line for the food and cleans off the table when leaving. It is a very non-threatening situation for everyone involved. However, are you secure in dining with a date in a formal restaurant on a special occasion? To help you, it is important to review proper dining etiquette while dating.

Be sure to make reservations if the restaurant is a fancy or popular one. It's very embarrassing to show up without reservations and have to wait for a table. This could leave a bad impression on your date. Some very fancy restaurants ask for your credit card number so don't be offended if this happens. Also, be sure and ask if a dress code is required. If a dress code is necessary, let your date know in advance and dress appropriately.

When being seated, do not allow the host or hostess to place you in unacceptable spots such as a noisy area, tables near a rest room, by the front or back door, areas with a bad atmosphere, etc. Politely ask the waiter who is seating you, "Is it possible that we can sit somewhere else, perhaps in the corner, there?" If he says no, do not argue and make a scene.

If you are at an upscale restaurant, you should order for your date. Ask her in advance what she wants and when your server comes, order for her. This will make a favorable impression on the young lady.

When your food arrives, eat at a moderate pace so that you will have time for conversation. It is poor etiquette to quickly eat your food and then spend the rest of the time watching your date finish his or her meal.

Don't slurp your soup, smack your lips, or chew with your mouth open. Nothing is more unsightly than watching someone talk and chew their food at the same time. Your napkin should be placed on your lap at all times. Don't tuck it into your belt or use it as a bib. If you have to get up, place it neatly on your seat. The rules of dining etiquette are simple to follow and will prevent much embarrassment.

When dining, pay attention to your date. Talk to your date; good eye contact is important. Try to smile once in awhile. Ask your date if her food is all right. If she needs anything, you are the one who is supposed to get the server's attention.

In most upscale restaurants, the waiter serves as your cashier unless the waiter tells you to pay the cashier or the check has written on it "Please pay cashier," then leave the tip on the table and stop at the cashier's desk to pay the check. Be sure to leave at least a 15% tip, more if the service was outstanding, less if the service was poor.

Review the section on table etiquette in this section of the LIFEPAC if you are unsure of your table manners, before you go on your date.

When going on a date, you will eventually encounter the dreaded time of ending the date. Often, this period will be full of tension as both of you are unsure of what to say and do. You can avoid this moment of tension by announcing to your date as you walk her to her door, that you "...hate to end the evening because you've had such a great time, but it is getting late and..." This will surprise and please her since most young men try to stall and prolong the saying goodbye hoping for a good night kiss. By ending the date you have perhaps set yourself apart from her former dates.

If this is your first date, you should assess how the date went. Answer the following questions truthfully and honestly.

1. Did the date go well? Did you have fun? If not, why? Lack of communication? Stage fright?

2. Did he/she seem to enjoy the evening?

3. Would you like to go out again? Remember to be honest with yourself. You are not obligated to go out on a second date. Neither is he/she.

FAMILY AND CONSUMER SCIENCE

seven

LIFEPAC TEST

80/100

Name _____

Date _____

Score _____

FAMILY AND CONSUMER SCIENCE 07: LIFEPAC TEST

Choose the correct letter (each answer, 4 points).

1. _____ is the common denominator for any party.
   a. Theme
   b. Decorations
   c. Food
   d. People

2. The _____ is the center of family life.
   a. home
   b. house
   c. TV room
   d. kitchen

3. The two priorities of the guest quarters are _____ .
   a. privacy and cleanliness
   b. clean linens and telephone
   c. bed and bathroom
   d. good food

4. The best way to see if the guest room is comfortable is to _____ .
   a. have guests fill out a questionnaire
   b. try it yourself
   c. Both a and b

5. _____ are the three main issues that come up in dating.
   a. How to accept the date, how to refuse the date, who pays
   b. Where to go on the date, what time to go on the date, who drives
   c. Who initiates the date, who controls the date, who pays

6. Bill keeps calling Ann trying to set up a date with her. Ann just doesn't care for Bill and is frustrated at his persistence. Ann can _____ .
   a. Make up an excuse, "Sorry I have to wash my hair that night."
   b. Be honest and tell him, "I don't think I'm the right girl for you, but I am flattered that you asked me."
   c. Say, "I'm not interested," and hang up on him.

7. David asked Mary on a date. Mary doesn't know if it is Dutch treat or if David is paying. Mary should _____ .
   a. take extra money with her on the date
   b ask David if he would like to go Dutch treat
   c. either a or b

8. When at a restaurant with good service, you should leave a _____ tip.
   a. 15%
   b. 20%
   c. 25%
   d. 10%

9. Tom is at a dinner and has food caught in his teeth. How can he properly remove it? _____
   a. Leave it, there is no polite way to pick food from your teeth.
   b. Excuse himself, go to the rest room and remove it.
   c. Use a toothpick and quickly remove it.

10. When guests at a motel are being loud and it is past midnight, you should _____ .
    a. bang on adjoining wall
    b. call the manager
    c. go talk to the offenders

11. The first step for cleaning the house is to _____ .
    a. dust
    b. vacuum
    c. neither a or b
    d. wash windows

12. You should have the oil changed in your car every _____ .
    a. 5,000 miles
    b. 3,000 miles
    c. 2,000 miles
    d. 2,500 miles

Define the following (6 points).

13. hospitality_____

    _____

    _____

Answer *true* **or** *false* (each answer, 2 points).

14. _____ Ten or less is a good number of guests for an evening of good conversation.

15. _____ A baby shower is an example of a party with a built-in theme.

16. _____ A shower is usually given by a family member.

17. _____ A thank you note is obligatory for an overnight stay.

18. _____ The best choice for a guest room would be the family room.

19. _____ A formal invitation should never be typed.

20. _____ When using eating utensils, work from the outside to the inside.

21. _____ It is acceptable to use your fingers to push food onto your fork.

22. _____ The meal begins when the hostess unfolds her napkin.

23. _____ It is inappropriate to go Dutch treat on a date; the young man should always pay.

24. _____ You need a reservation when dining at a fancy restaurant.

25. _____ A gentleman should **not** sit down at a formal dinner table until all ladies are seated.

26. _____ The theme provides continuity to a party.

27. _____ Cotton is the best fabric to use for dust cloths and cleaning rags.

28. _____ Citrus fruit rinds are used for getting rid of bad odors in the garbage disposal.

29. _____ A lemon wedge dipped in salt can remove rust stains from sinks and tubs.

30. _____ Evaluate your roof for replacement when it is five years old.

31. _____ Once the wallpaper has a tear in it, the whole room must be repapered.

2

32. _____ Use a plunger to fix a running toilet.

33. _____ Drive belts in your car's engine should have no more then a half inch give.

Write an essay (answer, 6 points).

34. Explain the steps in changing a tire.

_____

_____

_____

_____

_____

_____

_____

_____

_____

_____

Complete the following.

2.15 List the three main issues that come up during a date.

a. _____

b. _____

c. _____

2.16 Barry asks Sally to go to the football game with him on Friday. Sally really likes Barry, but already has a date to the game. What should she do? _____

_____

2.17 Gary keeps calling Molly, trying to set up a date with her. Molly just doesn't care for Gary and is frustrated at his persistence. What can she do? _____

_____

2.18 How many days in advance should you call to ask for a typical date? _____

2.19 What is the accepted method of asking someone on a date? _____

2.20 What information should John include when he asks Joyce out on a date? _____

_____

2.21 Bill asked Sue out on a date. Sue does not know if it is Dutch treat or if Bill is paying. What are her two options to this problem?

a. _____

b. _____

2.22 How can a young woman balance the financial obligations of dating if the young man pays all the time? _____

_____

2.23 Why is a reservation important at a fancy, upscale restaurant? _____

_____

2.24 Who would normally order the food at an upscale restaurant? _____

2.25 What is an appropriate tip? _____

 Review the material in this section in preparation for the Self Test. This Self Test will check your mastery of this particular section as well as your knowledge of the previous section.

SELF TEST 2

Choose the correct letter (each answer, 3 points).

2.01 Which of the following is not an appropriate gift for a couple's shower? _____
    a. towels   b. tools
    c. lingerie   d. housewares

2.02 Sam is at a formal dinner with Jill. Everyone is being seated at the table. Sam has assisted Jill in sitting down. He notices that Mary, who is to be sitting next to him on his other side, is still standing and her escort has already sat down. Which of the following is the best solution to Sam's dilemma? _____
    a. Sit down and hope that Mary's escort finally helps to seat her.
    b. Remain standing until Mary finally sits down.
    c. Assist Mary in sitting down.

2.03 Danny wants the salt and pepper. He sees it across the table in front of him. Which of the following should Danny do? _____
    a. Ask someone to pass the salt and pepper.
    b. Reach across the table and get the salt and pepper for himself.
    c. Wait for someone to pass the salt and pepper.

2.04 What is the signal that the meal has begun? _____
    a. The hostess unfolds her napkin.   b. The hostess takes her first bite of food.
    c. neither a nor b

2.05 Ann has discovered a cherry pit in her mouth. What should she do with it? _____
    a. Remove the pit with her thumb and forefinger.
    b. Spit the pit into her napkin.
    c. Place the pit on her fork and put it on the side of her plate.

2.06 Craig has food caught in his teeth. How can he properly remove it? _____
    a. Use a toothpick and quickly remove it.
    b. Excuse himself, go to the rest room and remove it.
    c. Turn his head away from the table and remove it.
    d. Leave it—there is no polite way to remove food from your teeth.

2.07 Tom is flying to Chicago to give a speech at a business conference. His seat mate is talking nonstop to him. Tom needs to polish his presentation for his meeting. What can Tom do about his talkative seat mate? _____
    a. Offer his seat mate a magazine or book.
    b. Tell his seat mate to "Be Quiet!"
    c. Ask the flight attendant to move him to another seat.

2.08 Tony is at a motel and the guests in another room are being really loud and it is almost midnight. What is the best thing for Tony to do? _____
    a. Bang on the adjoining wall.   b. Go talk to the offenders.
    c. Call the manager.   d. Call the police.

2.09   Chuck wants to take Kerry out for pizza but is short on funds. What would be the most appropriate plan of action? _____

    a. Call Kerry and honestly explain his money situation and ask her if she would mind going Dutch treat.

    b. Call Kerry and ask her to pay this time, promising that he will pay next time.

    c. Don't ask Kerry out.

Answer *true* **or** *false* (each answer, 2 points).

2.010   _____   Work from the outside to the inside when using eating utensils.

2.011   _____   Use the knife lying on the butter dish to spread butter on your bread.

2.012   _____   It is the job of the host to get the conversation rolling.

2.013   _____   Small talk is an effective way to fill voids in conversations.

2.014   _____   Cut all your meat at one time to limit unnecessary movement at the table.

2.015   _____   If you spill on the tablecloth, it is best to cover the spill with a plate or other object.

2.016   _____   It would be wise if a woman traveling alone carries a cellular phone.

2.017   _____   Make a reservation when dining at a fancy or upscale restaurant.

Fill in the blank (each answer, 4 points).

2.018   The two complaints most often made about air travelers are:

    a. _____

    b. _____

2.019   The _____ usually orders the food at an upscale restaurant.

2.020   You should leave a _____ % tip, unless the service is exceptional or is poor.

2.021   The two priorities for the guest quarters are:

    a. _____

    b. _____

2.022   Three main issues that come up in dating are:

    a. _____

    b. _____

    c. _____

2.023   The _____ is the center of family life.

2.024   The _____ provides continuity or unity to a party.

2.025   _____ is a comfortable number of guests for an evening of good conversation.

Short Answer (9 points).

2.026 Steve called Jane Monday night and asked her to go out for dinner Friday night. Jane happily accepted. Steve told her he would be driving his father's car and they would be double-dating with their friends, Bill and Marge. He told her they were going to Morton's Steak House, so she may want to dress up a little; similar to what she would wear to church.

Did Steve forget anything? _____ If so, what? _____

_____

80 / 100

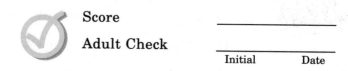

Score _____

Adult Check _____

Initial Date

III. HOME MANAGEMENT

With every privilege or gift comes responsibility. Taking care of what God has so richly blessed us with is an obligation and honor.

Nobody really likes housework—but a clean house creates a warm, welcoming, comfortable place for your family to live in and for friends to visit. Learning what tools and techniques to use when cleaning a house will make the task easier.

From time to time, your house will need a "face lift." Repairs and upkeep are essentials to maintain the good appearance and to extend the lifetime of your home.

If and when you are fortunate enough to own a car, you should be aware of the important responsibility of maintaining a smooth-running engine. Car maintenance increases the life of the car and decreases the strain on your finances. More importantly, it increases the safety for everyone when the car is in use.

In this section, you will have the opportunity to demonstrate your skills in household and automobile care and repair.

SECTION OBJECTIVES

Review these objectives. When you have completed this section, you should be able to:

8. Learn techniques used in household maintenance and repairs.

9. Demonstrate skill in housecleaning.

10. Learn techniques used in auto maintenance and repairs.

11. Demonstrate skill in selected auto care projects.

HOUSEHOLD MAINTENANCE AND REPAIR

It is easy to keep a clean house if you have the right tools.

Vacuum cleaner: An upright model with a powered beater-brush head works best on carpets. For hard-surface floors like wood or tile, use a floor nozzle attachment with a brush so you don't scratch the surface of the floor. Other attachments are usually included for cleaning upholstery, lamp shades, corners, under furniture, etc.

Portable, hand-held vacuums are convenient for quick spill cleanup but should not be your only vacuum.

Sponge mop: A sponge mop should have a replaceable sponge head.

Dust mop: The dust mop has a cotton head and is great for cleaning hard-surface floors.

Sponges: Get a variety of sponges in various sizes and textures for all kinds of cleaning tasks. Some may even have a scrub pad on one side which is very useful. Replace sponges when they start to smell or crumble away.

Cloths: Cotton cloths are best and are most absorbent.

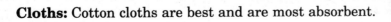

31

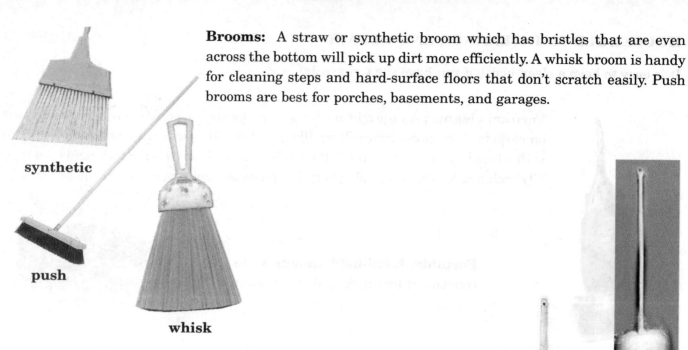

Brooms: A straw or synthetic broom which has bristles that are even across the bottom will pick up dirt more efficiently. A whisk broom is handy for cleaning steps and hard-surface floors that don't scratch easily. Push brooms are best for porches, basements, and garages.

synthetic

push

whisk

Dusters: A duster with a long handle will reach hard-to-get spots such as picture molding, tops of mirror frames, and light fixtures. You may choose between feather dusters and lamb's wool.

Buckets: You should have several buckets in various places in the house: bathroom, laundry room, kitchen, and garage.

Spray bottle: It is good to have several spray bottles on hand to fill with special need cleaners, such as spot removers, carpet cleaners, and water. Be sure to label each one clearly.

Squeegees: These are very effective for cleaning windows and large flat areas such as shower walls.

32

Various cleaners: An all-purpose spray-on cleaner is good to use on countertops and appliances. Use ammonia to cut grease, strip wax, and remove all types of soil. Use bleach to remove mildew and stubborn stains. Use heavy-duty scouring powders for porcelain sinks and tubs and soft-scrub cleansers for fiberglass, Formica®, and stainless steel. Waxes, polishes, and oil-based cleansers are used on wood, leather, brass, silver, copper, and other surfaces. Be sure to use the appropriate type of polish to avoid damaging a metal surface.

Dusting is the first step in cleaning a room. In order to dust properly, you will need cotton dust rags; a duster; a bottle of dusting spray, and furniture polish. Check the ceiling for cobwebs. Begin dusting as high as you can reach and work down to floor level. Dust mirrors and picture frames. Check walls for fingerprints and marks; wipe with cleaner and rag. Dust the horizontal surfaces of the furniture first, then the sides and legs. Be sure to lift any table ornaments up and dust them also. Use a duster to dust plants, window sills and frames, shades, and shutters. Don't forget the telephone, bookshelves, light fixtures, lampshades, rungs of chairs, baseboards, heat vents, tops of curtains and molding, computers, and electronic equipment, all of which attract dust.

Polishing wood will help to nourish it. Do not use liquid or spray polishes containing silicone or acrylic resin on antique wood as they will seal the surface. Most wooden furniture tends to be varnished, lacquered, or waxed. Always wipe a wood surface with a damp, lint-free cloth before polishing to remove dust and grime, or the polishing action will simply grind them in. Apply polish to furniture and buff in the direction of the wood grain using a clean, soft cloth or duster. Oiled wood has a soft, low sheen and should not be polished. Instead, use a wood oil applied sparingly with a soft cloth. Rub this in the directions of the grain and gently buff to a luster using a clean, soft cloth.

HOW TO DUST	
Venetian blinds and mini-blinds	Use a feather duster and wipe with cloth.
CDs/DVDs	Wipe with soft cloth.
Computer	Wipe screen with soft cloth and screen cleanser.
Books	Dust with feather duster, wipe with soft cloth or vacuum with small brush attachments. Use soft white bread or gum eraser to remove grease spots. Rub gently, being careful not to damage the pages.
Sofas and chairs	Use your vacuum cleaner.
Framed pictures	Use cloth and glass cleanser.
Lampshades	Dust with feather duster then finish up with brush attachment of vacuum.
Oil Paintings	Dust with feather duster then wipe with soft, clean cloth.
Plants	Wipe leaves with a clean cloth. You can put small or medium-size plants in the tub or out in the rain for a thorough cleansing or use a garden hose.
Shutters	Vacuum, then wipe with damp rag or sponge.
Audio or CD player	Wipe with soft cloth.
Television, Video Player	Wipe with soft cloth or vacuum with small brush attachment. Clean TV screen with cleanser or soap, then rinse with clean, damp rag or sponge and buff dry with soft, clean cloth.
Telephone	Wipe with damp rag or sponge and cleaning liquid.

When you vacuum, be sure to allow enough time to pick up the dirt; let the vacuum nozzle linger on each section and move it back and forth to ensure that you pick up all the particles. Pay special attention to high-traffic areas such as hallways, doorways, and around chairs and sofas. In order to do a thorough job you may have to move some furniture. Remember, it is best to vacuum hard-surface floors before you mop them. Area rugs can also be vacuumed; it might be easier to take small rugs outside and shake them.

If your hard-surface floor is no-wax vinyl, hardwood treated with polyurethane varnish, or ceramic tile, fill one bucket with ammonia (about 1/4 to 1/2 cup) and water and another bucket with plain water. Wipe the ammonia solution over the floor with the mop. Let the solution sit for a few minutes, then mop it back up. Rinse with the plain water. You may have to rinse more than once if the floor was extremely dirty. A word of caution: if the grout in your ceramic tile is not sealed, mopping your floor as described above could leave the grout discolored or dingy looking. You may want to clean each tile separately to maintain good, clean grout. For waxed floors or wood floors you will need specialty cleaners and methods.

Walls, whether painted, paneled, or papered, should be cleaned a few times a year, particularly in kitchens and bathrooms, as they accumulate grease and dust. In between washings you can vacuum your walls using the large brush attachment. This gets rid of dust and can be done quickly.

Regular vacuuming is the best way to maintain your carpets and rugs, but every so often you will find that the carpet needs a thorough cleaning. You can either rent equipment and "shampoo" your carpets yourself or you can hire professionals to come into your home and do the job. You can do spot cleaning on heavily soiled areas between shampooing using the foam or powder carpet cleaners; apply them, rub them in, and then vacuum up the residue.

Regular vacuuming of upholstered furniture is very important. You can use the upholstery or brush attachment on your vacuum to do this. You can also remove surface dirt using a clean cloth dampened with carpet shampoo.

When washing windows, use vertical motions on one side of the window and horizontal motions on the other side of the window, that way you will be able to tell which side the streaks are on. Wash from top to bottom. Use an ammonia solution or white vinegar solution to wash windows. Use a long-handled, wide blade squeegee on large windows. It is best to wash windows on a cloudy or overcast day because the sun causes the windows to dry too fast and then streak.

Clean window screens with the brush attachment of your vacuum or a brush-type paint roller.

Practical, Inexpensive Household Cleaning Solutions

The Kitchen

1. Water stains on faucet	Mix vinegar and baking soda together in a bowl and apply the mixture liberally to the fixture. Wipe off with a clean damp cloth.
2. Clean counters	Using warm water, wipe with an old cotton shirt or sponge. For stubborn areas use club soda or lemon juice.
3. Clean stainless steel sink	Remove spots with vinegar first, then apply club soda. Be sure to dry afterwards or the club soda will dry as new spots.
4. Garbage disposal smell	Place rind from citrus fruit and turn on the disposal. Or a large amount of ice cubes heavily dosed with vinegar.
5. Clean cupboards	Wash out with a damp cloth dipped in vinegar water. Line with shelf paper. Keep your cupboards neat and organized.
6. Refrigerators	Clean with soapy water and rinse well. To get rid of odors, place an open box of baking soda inside.

Bathroom

1. Tracks of shower doors	Scrub with an old toothbrush and bleach. Be sure to do this before you clean the floor or tub.
2. Ring around the toilet	Use an acid cleanser and scrub. If that doesn't work use sandpaper or a moist pumice stone. Be careful–some porcelain will not take that kind of cleaning.
3. Faucet stains	Vinegar and hot water.
4. Rust stain on sinks and tubs below faucet	Cut a wedge of lemon and put salt on it. Rub it onto the rust stain. Use a wet cloth to rinse it off.
5. Soap scum on sinks and tubs	Soap scum is actually similar to a grease so use a degreaser.

Bedrooms

1. The bed	Make your bed every day and change bedding once a week. This will give your room a neater appearance and fresher smell.
2. Nightstand	Clear off the clutter from the nightstand to give your bedroom a neater appearance.
3. Plants	Dust your plants. A clean plant can help clean the air in the room.
4. Odors	Use deodorizer for shoes. Use a hamper for dirty clothes. Light a few scented candles for atmosphere as well as freshening the air.

Complete the following.

3.1   What type of vacuum cleaner works best on carpet? _____

3.2   List two types of brooms available.

     a. _____

     b. _____

3.3   What type of fabric is best for cloths? _____ Why? _____
_____

3.4   What is a squeegee and what is it used for? _____
_____

3.5   What is the first step in cleaning a room? _____ Where does one begin? _____
_____

3.6   How do you dust the TV screen? _____

3.7   In what directional motion do you polish and buff furniture? _____

3.8   When you vacuum, allow enough _____ to pick up the dirt.

3.9   What is the best way to maintain your carpets and rugs? _____

3.10   When washing windows how can you decide on which side are the streaks? _____
_____

3.11   For the removal of stains on a faucet, you may use a mixture of _____ and
_____ .

3.12   Citrus fruit rinds are used for _____ .

3.13   A _____ and _____ can remove rust stains on sinks and tubs.

Complete the following activity.

3.14   There are many tasks that must be done every day and others perhaps only once a year. You need to make a schedule that will best organize your household cleaning tasks. What follows is a general schedule. It should serve as a starting point for your own personal chart. Your house may have special tasks such as fireplace cleaning, chimney sweeping, wood floors to be varnished and/or polished, stair rails that need dusting, etc. Note there as been space left in each square for you to add your special tasks. Have your teacher check your revised chart.

Making a Cleaning Schedule: Daily/Weekly/Monthly/Seasonal Tasks				
Room	**Daily**	**Weekly**	**Monthly**	**Seasonal**
Bedroom	Make beds Put clothing away Arrange dresser top	Change bed Vacuum Dust furniture Empty trash	Organize closets and drawers Air pillows Dust lamps	Clean closets Wash blankets Wash windows Clean screens
Bathroom	Clean sink and tub Replace dirty towels Empty trash basket	Wash floor Clean toilet Wipe tile surfaces Clean mirrors	Wash shower curtain Wash walls Wash rugs Organize cabinets	Clean cabinets Wash windows Clean screens
Kitchen	Wash dishes Clean range top Wipe counters Empty garbage Clean floor Clean sink	Clean microwave Dispose of leftovers Wipe refrigerator Wash floor	Clean refrigerator and freezer Clean oven Wax floor Scrub trash can	Clean cabinets Wash stored dishes Wash windows Clean screens
Living Room	Dispose of papers Arrange magazines and ornaments	Vacuum rugs Dust, polish furniture Dust, clean lamps	Shampoo rugs Clean under furniture Clean mirrors	Clean closets Wash windows Clean screens Wash walls

Adult Check _____

                    Initial   **Date**

Basic tools. Being able to confidently deal with simple household repairs is an important part of running a home with minimum fuss and expense. Many common problems such as leaky faucets, blocked drains, and squeaky doors are often easy to remedy if you are prepared.

Being prepared means having the right tools for each task. Buy tools as you need them instead of the packaged sets. Buy high quality tools; good tools not only encourage you to do good work, they make for a safer work environment.

Sandpaper
(keep a variety of grits)
and sand block

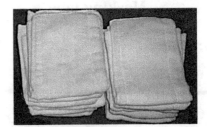

Rags

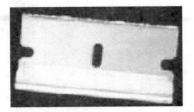

Single-edge razor blade

Pencil

Steel wool

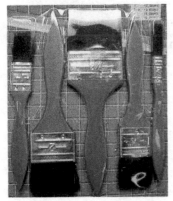

Standard paint brushes

Grounded
extension
cord (if you
need it for
outside,
make sure it
is intended
for that use)

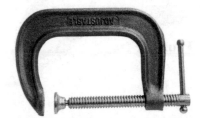

Fasteners such as straps,
clamps, and vises

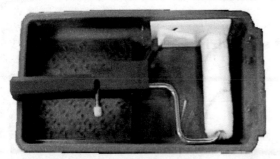

Paint roller, paint pans
or buckets

Wire brush

Masking tape

Duct tape

Level

Putty knife

Adjustable wrench

Scissors

Plunger

Retractable rule or tape measure

Phillips screwdriver

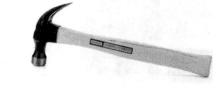
Curved claw hammer

Slip-joint pliers

Flat-head screwdriver

Pipe wrench

Plumb line

Stepladder

Locking grip pliers

Dustpan

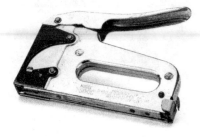
Staple gun

Whisk broom

Power tools such as electric drills, screwdrivers, and saws make the work easier and the project go more quickly.

Picture the exterior of your home without any kind of surface finish. Not only would it look unattractive but it would be unprotected against the elements. The most popular exterior finishes are paint, **shingles**, stucco, and aluminum or vinyl siding. Obviously, your home needs repair if paint is peeling or shingles are falling off. The roof of your home will probably need to be replaced every 10-15 years, depending on the type of roof you have and where you live.

Exterior Maintenance Schedule

Spring
- ✔ Recaulk joints between siding and other materials.
- ✔ Check window sills for debris.
- ✔ Check all wood surfaces for paint failure and damage.
- ✔ Nail down loose siding and trim; replace decayed sections.
- ✔ Wash vinyl, aluminum or painted-wood siding.
- ✔ Check deck or patio for loose boards, bricks or stones.
- ✔ Check roof for damaged shingles.
- ✔ Inspect flashing at chimney, dormers, vents, and skylights.
- ✔ Clean gutters, downspout, and leaf strainers; check for damage and paint failure.
- ✔ Evaluate a roof that is 15 years or older for replacement.
- ✔ Clean screens and check for damage.
- ✔ Replace worn or damaged weather stripping.

Fall
- ✔ Check for bird nests in chimneys and vents.
- ✔ Apply new caulking around windows and doors if needed.

The largest jobs for the maintenance and repair of the interior of your home are the flooring, walls, and ceiling. Keeping these areas in top condition will be your best defense against wear and tear. Shampooing, stripping and waxing, and painting will be the main tasks. Sometimes you may need to repair small holes in the wall with a little plaster and paint. Maybe you will have to patch a tear in the wallpaper.

The most common problem with older windows and doors is swelling and warping due to humidity. If the door sticks, find the exact spot by pushing or pulling lightly at parts of the closed door. The sticky area will resist your efforts. Once you've located the spot, look for wear, scratches, and worn paint. You need to either **plane** or sand the area, being careful not to take too much off. When the door no longer sticks, you can refinish the area with paint or varnish.

Most problems with faucets and toilets are usually easily fixed. Here are some common problems and how to fix them.

Meager flow from faucet. Unscrew the nozzle, take the washer out and inspect for wear. If it is worn, replace it. Check the **aerator** screen for wear. If there is no wear, only built-up soap scum, soak the aerator in a vinegar and water solution until clean.

Running toilets. The most common problem occurs because the **flapper** is not blocking the flush valve, so water keeps filling the tank. Check to see if something is blocking the flapper or if the chain is tangled. Also, check the flapper for wear. If the chain and flapper are worn, replace them.

Overflowing toilets. The first thing to do is turn off the water valve. The water valve can be turned off at the base of the toilet against the wall. If you need to shut off the entire water source to your house, the valve is generally out in the front yard or in the basement. Have a parent show you where this is located for emergencies.

Dripping faucets and sinks. The water shut-off valves are below the individual sinks. There are two valves, one for the cold water and one for the hot water. If you need to shut off the entire water source to your house, the valve is generally out in the front yard. Have a parent show you where this is located.

Handle problems. If the toilet handle sticks or conversely, is loose, you will need to adjust the chain and possibly clean the handle mounting nut. Use a vinegar solution to remove lime deposits.

Clogged drain. The basic method is to pour boiling or extremely hot water down the drain. If this does not work, use a plunger. Position it over the drain and push down forcefully three times. When the plunger is removed, the water should rush down. If not, repeat. If this does not work, you may have to rent or buy a plumber's snake. For clogged toilets, use a plunger as well.

There are other quick repair jobs that might arise from time to time. Some of these include: applying new caulking around sinks and tubs, adjusting and oiling garage door opener, spraying and trapping for pest control, repairing small appliances, replacing damaged cords or switches on lamps, changing fuses or defective circuit breakers, dealing with burst or frozen pipes, and many, many more.

As you can see, there is a great deal of responsibility in owning a home. Proper care and repair of your home will give you great satisfaction and a sense of achievement. Your home will have a longer life and beauty because of your efforts.

Answer the following.

3.15 Evaluate your roof for replacement when it is _____ .

3.16 The most popular exterior finishes for houses are _____ , _____ ,

_____ , and _____ or _____ .

3.17 *True* or *False*. Once the wallpaper has a tear in it, the whole room must be repapered. _____

3.18 Why would you have to plane or sand a spot on a door? _____

_____

3.19 Why check the aerator screen of the faucet? _____

_____

3.20 What is the most common problem that occurs when the toilet won't stop running? _____

_____

3.21 What solution best gets rid of lime deposits? _____

3.22 What is a plunger used for? _____

Complete the following activity.

3.23 Walk through your home and inspect it for needed repairs. Make a list of the needed repairs. Beside each task write what needs to be done to make those repairs and what tools and supplies are needed to accomplish each task.

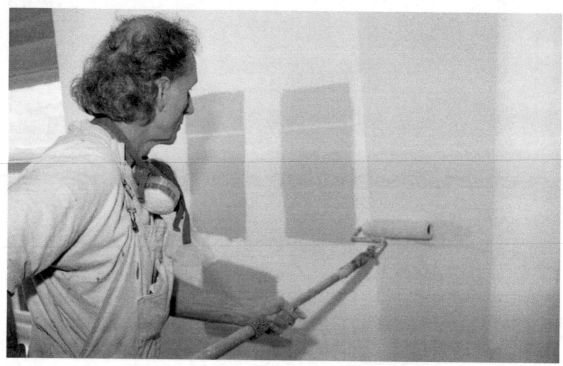

Your house may need a fresh coat of paint.

REPAIR NEEDS AT MY HOME		
Task	Supplies	How to repair
Example: peeling caulking around bathroom sink.	Tube of caulking	Remove all old caulking. Apply new caulking according to directions on package.

Adult Check _____

Initial   Date

Keeping the interior of your car clean and free of clutter is as much a safety issue as it is an appearance issue. Did you know that an object—a book, for example—that might be thrown against the back of your head in an accident can be as lethal as a bullet to the head? It is important for you to keep your car clutter free. Whenever you clean out your car, be sure to remove anything that you don't need. After all, your car can't look as clean and as new if there is a lot of junk littering the seats and floors.

The top of the dashboard of almost every car on the road today is made out of some kind of vinyl. There are two things you should do to keep your dashboard looking new and prevent it from drying out. First, you can purchase a fabric or carpet dashboard cover that can be easily cleaned with a vacuum cleaner. Second, you should clean the dashboard every few weeks with soap and warm water and after each cleaning give it a good rub down with a vinyl treatment that can be purchased at most drug and auto parts stores. This will keep the vinyl moist and help prevent it from cracking.

Keep the seats in the car clean. Leather seats may be washed in warm, soapy water and then treated with saddle soap or a leather treatment product. Cloth seats should be vacuumed weekly. You can clean dirty spots or stains with warm, soapy water and/or stain removers.

The carpets of the car should be vacuumed weekly and cleaned when they get dirty. Be sure to open the windows when drying wet carpets so the car won't smell like mildew. A real asset to every car is a set of floor mats. It is the best way to protect the actual carpet from wear and tear.

The best and easiest way to clean car windows is to spray them with a window cleaner and dry with a newspaper, wiping in a circular motion to avoid streaking.

There are many choices of car deodorizers available to keep your car smelling fresh and clean. These can be found at auto stores, drug stores, or any other store that sells auto parts.

Don't forget the trunk. Keep it clean and clutter free also. Vacuum it every time you clean you car or whenever it gets soiled.

The exterior of the car should be washed with warm, soapy water then rinsed with a garden hose. It is good to use a spray gun nozzle on the hose to get more force for removing the dirty water. After you have dried the car with soft cotton rags, use a **chamois** to get any spots that you missed. To protect your car's paint job from the elements, you might want to wax it.

There are a number of cleaning products available for your car. A few of these products and their functions are listed.

- ☿ **Vinyl/leather cleaner**—If you car has vinyl or leather seats, then this item is essential. There is no way to restore vinyl or leather to its original glossy sheen unless you use this type of product.

- ☿ **Tire cleanser**—You can buy special detergents made for getting the dirt off tires.

- ☿ **Silicone spray**—This item is used to keep rubber from getting cracked and brittle, such as the seals around your window.

- ⊛ **Tar removing cleanser**—This detergent is specifically designed to get sticky tar spots from highways and roads off of your car.

- ⊛ **Polish**—This is the agent that gives your car's paint job a showroom shine.

- ⊛ **Stain remover**—Use a conventional furniture stain remover to clean stubborn stains from your cloth seats.

▰ **Answer the following questions.**

3.24   Why is it important to keep your car clutter-free? _____

3.25   Two things will help keep your dashboard looking new are _____ and
        _____ .

3.26   How often should you vacuum the carpets in the car? _____

3.27   How should you clean your car's windows? _____

        Why? _____

3.28   What can you use on your car's exterior paint to protect it from the elements? _____

3.29   What would you use silicone spray for on your car? _____

▰ **Complete the following activity.**

3.30   Wash and clean the interior and exterior of the family car.

⊘ **Adult Check** _____
                       Initial   Date

By spending about fifteen minutes each month making the following checks, you will save hundreds of dollars in repairs and increase the life of your car.

> **Special note to the ladies:** You may never plan on having the responsibility of servicing the car yourself. You may use a mechanic for this job. You still need to know what the mechanic is supposed to be doing and check to see that he has done a complete and honest job. Many people have experienced engine replacements due to dishonest mechanics who failed to change the oil, even though they said they had. Watch them work if you can and then check the dipstick, fluid reservoirs, etc. yourself.

✔ **Check the coolant.** It is in a plastic reservoir next to the radiator with marks that say "Full Hot" and "Full Cold." If the coolant level is below the "Full Cold" mark, add water to bring it up. Or you can add antifreeze in cold weather for extra protection.

If the car is hot, do not open the radiator cap. Pressure and heat escaping can cause severe burns. Wait till the car cools down.

If the car is hot, don't open the radiator cap.

✔ **Check the brakes.** A really simple way to check power brakes is to press down on the brake pedal while the engine is running. If the pedal stops firmly about halfway down and stays there, then the brakes are fine. If the pedal stop is mushy or the pedal keeps going to the floor, you may need brake work.

Checking the brake fluid on most new cars is also very easy. Check your owner's manual for the fluid reservoir's location. Add the recommended fluid only to the level indicated.

Check engine oil

✔ **Check the oil.** First, turn off the engine. Find the oil dipstick under the hood. If the car has been running, be careful since the dipstick will be hot. Pull the dipstick out, clean it off, reinsert it and pull it out again. Notice the oil level. "Full" and "Add" are marked on the end of the stick. If the oil level is between the two marks you are OK. If it is below "Add," add enough oil to reach the "Full" line. Usually it will take one quart of oil to raise the level from the "Add" to the "Full" line.

To add oil, remove the cap at the top of the engine. You may have to add more than one quart. Check your owner's manual or the sticker from your last oil change for the recommended type and weight of oil.

Changing your oil regularly—every 3,000 miles—is the single most important way to protect your engine. You should change the oil filter whenever you change the oil. If the oil light comes on the dashboard, pull over and stop the car immediately or you might seriously damage the motor.

✔ **Check transmission fluid.** An automatic transmission is complicated and very expensive to replace. Checking your transmission fluid level can prevent costly repair. First find the transmission fluid dipstick. (It is usually at the back of the engine and looks like the oil dipstick but smaller.) The engine should be warmed up and running. If fluid is below the "Add" line, pour in one pint at a time. Your owner's manual will tell you the correct type of transmission fluid for your car. Do not over fill the reservoir.

✔ **Keep the tires inflated.** Improper inflation is the major cause for premature tire failure. Check your tire pressure at least once a month. The owner's manual will tell you the most fuel-efficient inflation. Buy a good tire gauge since the ones at a service station are not generally reliable. You should be able to change a tire. Your owner's manual will have complete instructions showing you how to change a tire.

How to change a tire.

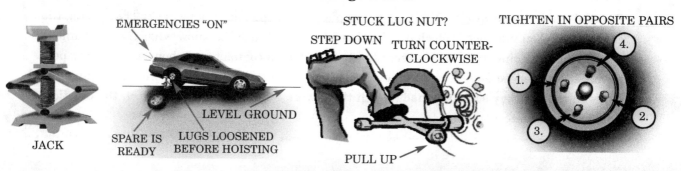

JACK   EMERGENCIES "ON"   LEVEL GROUND   SPARE IS READY   LUGS LOOSENED BEFORE HOISTING   STUCK LUG NUT?   STEP DOWN   TURN COUNTER-CLOCKWISE   PULL UP   TIGHTEN IN OPPOSITE PAIRS

Changing a Flat Tire

- ✔ Park on a level surface, activate hazard flashers, and set the parking brake.
- ✔ Place gearshift lever in P (Park).
- ✔ Block the diagonally opposite wheel.
- ✔ Use the tip of the lug wrench to remove any wheel trim (hub cap, etc.).
- ✔ Loosen each wheel lug nut, but do not remove them until the wheel is raised up off the ground.
- ✔ Position the jack according to the directions. Turn the jack handle clockwise until the tire is raised approximately 1″ off the ground.
- ✔ Remove the lug nuts with the lug wrench. Replace the flat tire with the spare tire.
- ✔ Reinstall the lug nuts, cone side in, until the wheel is snug against the hub. Do not fully tighten the lug nuts until the wheel has been lowered.
- ✔ Lower the wheel by turning the jack handle counterclockwise.
- ✔ Remove the jack and fully tighten the lug nuts.
- ✔ Replace all wheel trim.

✔ **Check your power steering fluid.** If your car has power steering, this also requires fluid. Checking the fluid will prevent major repair bills. The power steering fluid reservoir is connected by a belt to the engine. Unscrew the cap and look into the reservoir. There will be markings inside. Replace fluid to the indicated marking if it is low.

✔ **Keep drive belts taut.** A loose drive belt in your engine can lead to electrical problems, cooling problems, even air conditioning problems. To check the belt tension, push down on the middle of each drive belt. It should feel tight. If you can push down more than half an inch, the belt needs tightening.

Also check that each belt is in good condition. Frayed edges or tears indicate the belt could break at any time. Replace it immediately.

An alternator

✔ **Check the battery.** If your battery has caps on top, lift each one off and check that the fluid comes to the bottom of the filler neck. If it doesn't, add distilled water. Be careful. The fluid is an acid. Look for corrosion around the connections. This can prevent electrical circuits from being completed, leading you to assume your perfectly good battery is dead.

If cables are corroded, remove them and clean with fine sandpaper or steel wool. The inside of the connection and the battery posts should be shiny when you put the cables back on.

✔ **Change the air filter.** This is probably the easiest item to maintain. Simply look at it; if it looks dirty, change it.

✔ **Check the windshield wipers.** If the windshield wipers are brittle or cracked, they need to be replaced. Wiper blades that are in poor condition can make it more difficult to see because of the terrible streaks they leave. The way to prevent this is by keeping the wiper blades clean. They are made of exactly the same rubber material that is found in the seals around your windows. As such, they should be regularly cleaned with silicone spray to prevent them from cracking. Be sure that the window cleaner reservoir is full for those in-between cleaning emergencies.

Examples of air filters

✔ **Check the external lights.** You should pay close attention to the lights on your car. They are, besides your horn, the only means of communicating to other drivers. Keep them clean and in working condition. It is especially important that your brake lights work Usually if they are not working it is a simple matter of changing the bulb.

Once again you understand the big responsibility involved in owning a car. Keeping your car in good repair will guarantee everyone a more enjoyable and safer experience.

**Wiper blades need to be changed.
Keep car lights clean and maintained.**

Answer the following questions.

3.31 Which five reservoirs should you check on your car?

a. _____   d. _____

b. _____   e. _____

c. _____

3.32 How can you tell if the brakes on your car need work? _____

_____

_____

3.33 What should you do first after removing the oil dipstick from the car? _____

_____

3.34 How often should you have the oil changed in your car? _____

_____

3.35 If a drive belt has more than _____ give, the belt needs tightening.

3.36 How does corrosion around the connections of a battery affect its working ability? _____

_____

3.37 How can you tell that the air filter needs to be changed? _____

3.38 What is the problem most likely to be if the car lights are not working? _____

_____

Complete the following activity.

3.39 Give the family car a thorough service check by using the checklist guide. With the permission of your parents, make the necessary repairs to keep the car running efficiently.

⊘ **Adult Check** _____
                    Initial   Date

50

Before you take this last Self Test, you may want to do one or more of these self checks.

1. _____ Read the objectives. Determine if you can do them.

2. _____ Restudy the material related to any objectives that you cannot do.

3. _____ Use the SQ3R study procedure to review the material:
   a. **S**can the sections.
   b. **Q**uestion yourself again (review the questions you wrote initially).
   c. **R**ead to answer your questions.
   d. **R**ecite the answers to yourself.
   e. **R**eview areas you didn't understand.

4. _____ Review all vocabulary, activities and Self Tests, writing a correct answer for each wrong answer.

SELF TEST 3

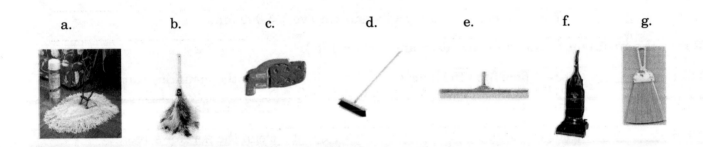

a.   b.   c.   d.   e.   f.   g.

Using the items above match each item (each answer, 3 points).

3.01 _____ work best for carpets

3.02 _____ for cleaning windows

3.03 _____ for cleaning hard-surfaced floors

3.04 _____ feather or lamb's wool

3.05 _____ for sweeping steps

3.06 _____ for sweeping porches, basements, and garages

3.07 _____ for quick spill cleanup

Answer *true* **or** *false* (each answer, 2 points).

3.08 _____ The first step in cleaning your house is to vacuum.

3.09 _____ The best way to clean venetian blinds is to feather dust and wipe with a clean cloth.

3.010 _____ Buff furniture in the direction of the wood grain.

3.011 _____ It is not necessary to vacuum hard-surface floors before you mop them.

3.012 _____ Regular vacuuming is the best way to maintain your carpets.

3.013 _____ When washing windows, use vertical motions on one side of the window and horizontal motions on the other side.

3.014 _____ Vinegar and baking soda make a good solution for cleaning water stains on faucets.

3.015 _____ A lemon wedge and baking soda are used to remove rust stains.

3.016 _____ Make your bed daily.

3.017 _____ Evaluate your roof for replacement after the first five years.

3.018 _____ Improper tire inflation is the major cause of tire failures.

3.019 _____ Humidity can cause older windows and doors to swell.

3.020 _____ A vinegar solution is best for getting rid of lime deposits.

3.021 _____ One way to keep the dashboard of your car from cracking is to rub petroleum jelly on it.

3.022 _____ The best way to clean car windows is with newspapers.

3.023 _____ The oil should be changed in your car every 5,000 miles.

Match the problem to the solution (each answer, 3 points).

3.024 _____ meager flow from the faucet   a. clean the mounting nut

3.025 _____ running toilets   b. check the flapper

3.026 _____ a clogged drain   c. clean the aerator screen

3.027 _____ toilet handle problems   d. silicone spray

3.028 _____ stuck door   e. plunger

3.029 _____ cracking rubber seals around windows   f. plane or sand

Short Answer (each answer, 4 points).

3.030 Give one example of a housecleaning task that needs to be done seasonally.

_____

3.031 Why, besides appearance, is it important to keep your car clutter free?

_____

_____

Complete the following (each answer, 4 points).

3.032 List four maintenance checks for your car.

a. _____

b. _____

c. _____

d. _____

Write an essay (5 points).

3.033   Explain the process or steps in checking the oil.

_____

_____

_____

_____

_____

_____

_____

_____

_____

_____

_____

_____

_____

_____

<table>
<tr><td>80</td></tr>
<tr><td>100</td></tr>
</table>

Score   _____

Adult Check   _____

Initial   Date

Before taking the LIFEPAC Test, you may want to do one or more of these self checks.

1. _____   Read the objectives. Check to see if you can do them.
2. _____   Restudy the material related to any objectives that you cannot do.
3. _____   Use the SQ3R study procedure to review the material.
4. _____   Review activities, Self Tests, and LIFEPAC vocabulary words.
5. _____   Restudy areas of weakness indicated by the last Self Test.

GLOSSARY

aerator. An apparatus that adds air to the water so that it spreads out when it flows from the faucet.

brioche. A light, sweet bun or roll made with eggs, yeast, and butter.

chamois. A special type of polishing cloth made out of a soft leather. It is used during the final stages of drying your car.

caulk. To seal or close a seam to make it watertight, airtight; to prevent leakage.

debutante. A young woman making her formal entrance into society.

decorum. Proper behavior, speech, and dress.

dormer. A roofed structure containing a vertically-set window.

dutch treat. A meal or other entertainment where each person pays his way.

flapper. A broad, flat hinged piece that closes over the toilet tank drain.

53

flashing. Sheet metal or a similar object used to cover and protect certain joints and angles, such as where a roof comes in contact with a wall.

grits. The abrasive particles on the surface of sandpaper; they may be fine, medium, or coarse.

grounded. The ground wire is common to all wires in the house, it protects against short circuits and shocks from current surges.

harassed. Persistently troubled, tormented, pestered.

initiate. Begin, get going, get started.

maraca. A gourd or a gourd-shaped rattle filled with seeds or pebbles and used, often as a pair, as a rhythm instrument. They are often decoratively painted with bright colors.

Mariachis. A group of performers that sing and play Mexican-style songs.

piñata. A gaily decorated crock or papier-mache figure filled with small toys, candy, etc., and suspended above, so that blindfolded children may break it or knock it down with sticks and scramble for the contents. Used especially for birthdays and Christmas festivals.

plane. A tool that smooths or shaves a thin layer off the surface of wood.

platonic. A close relationship between a male and female which doesn't involve romantic feelings.

plumb line. A cord with a metal bob attached to one end and used to determine perpendicularity, the depth of water, etc.

putty knife. A broad-bladed tool for spreading putty which is a substance used for filling cracks in drywall or wood.

shingles. A thin piece of wood, slate, metal, similar substance; usually oblong, laid in overlapping rows to cover the roofs and walls of buildings.

thermography. A process of writing or printing involving the use of heat; especially a raised printing process in which matter printed by letterpress is dusted with powder and heated to make the lettering rise.

BIBLIOGRAPHY

Craig, Betty, *Don't Slurp Your Soup*, Brighten Publishers Inc., MN, 1991

Jones, Beneth Peters, *Beauty and the Best*, Bob Jones University Press, Greenville, SC, paperback, 1988.

King, June, *Helpful Household Hints*, Santa Monica press CA, 1996.

Lefever, Marlene, *Creative Hospitality*, Tyndale House Publishers, IL, 1980.

Pistole, Elizabeth, *Serving With Love*, Warner Press, MN, 1979.

Pittman, Grace, *Hospitality With Confidence*, Bethany House Publishers, MN, 1986.

Post, Elizabeth L. and Coles, Joan M., *Emily Post's Teen Etiquette*, Harper Perennial, 1995.

The Illustrated Hints, Tips and Household Skills, SMITHMARK Publishers, Inc., NY, 1995.

Tuckerman, Nancy, *The Amy Vanderbilt Complete Book of Etiquette*, Doubleday, NY, 1995.

Wissenger, Joanna, *The Home Answer Book,* Harper Collins Publishers, NY, 1995